THE (

OF OPEN

TRANSFORMING YOUR BUSINESS THROUGH TRANSPARENCY, TRUTH, AND TRUST

NICK BERG

THE CULTURE OF OPEN
Transforming Your Business
Through Transparency, Truth, and Trust

Nick Berg
NSB Publishing
Copyright © 2016
All rights reserved.

ISBN-13: 978-0692659915
ISBN-10: 0692659919

Printed in the United States of America

THE CULTURE OF OPEN

INTRODUCTION

"We are at times too ready to believe that the present is the only possible state of things."

Marcel Proust

THE TERM "OPEN" IS RICH WITH MEANING AND POSITIVE connotations. Among other things, it is associated with candor, freedom, flexibility, expansiveness, engagement, sharing and access. However, it is not an adjective that has traditionally been used to describe corporations. Adjectives like insular, bureaucratic, hierarchical, secretive, and closed are more synonymous with companies—especially large establishments.

Over the course of my career, I've worked with many different organizations and observed business processes and how those businesses have changed and transformed their cultures. Initially, this transformation into a "Culture of Open" began with computer systems.

However, over time, the benefits of being more open have become more apparent, not only in the information technology industry, but in other organizations and industries as well. As these open cultures have evolved and the benefits of having an open culture have grown, it has become more and more apparent that a closed culture can be an inhibitor to organization realizing growth in both business innovation and profits.

Over the years a common thread came out of my observations and experiences, and I became convinced that the more open companies are, the more easily they are transformed and able to accept change—and the more profitable they become.

I have worked in both closed and open cultures. I started my career with the US Army. As is the case with most military organizations, that culture was very closed. Of course most military organizations require some degree of secrecy, yet it still became apparent to me that the best intelligence often came through open sources, such as television, newspapers, books, and people. Even the openness of the Internet provided a greater wealth of information than other sources.

Working for a year with IBM in Saudi Arabia, which was a closed culture, made it even more apparent that sources and information that were open were much more reliable. I found that the organizational seclusion in those countries became a roadblock to progress because they didn't know what technological innovations and organizational advancements were happening in the world.

It became clear to me while working with companies in the Middle East that closed cultures often presented or created problems. In trying to resolve those problems, occasions came into play that gave me an opportunity to introduce an open-culture style and other ways people could change, in order to remove these obstacles.

I've witnessed the benefits of an open culture to companies, especially via open-source software and project management, two primary focus areas in my career. The concept of a Culture of Open initially piqued my interest when I was writing my first book on project management. I realized that there was value in being open and understanding about projects. Rather than limiting or hindering a company's ability to profit and succeed, an open culture can spur innovation and not only increase about projects, but also increase exposure, quality, and performance. Being open doesn't decrease value; it improves value.

Often business practices are very closed: bid processes cannot be disclosed; companies closely guard their (USP) unique selling proposition; and corporations don't allow their vendors to communicate with each other.

As I managed projects and served as an advisor to the top 50 companies in the Fortune 500 in the US, I was able to convince them that they needed to make some of their processes transparent. As a result, they were able to drive the business process from idea to market more quickly, facilitate faster institutional change, and accelerate the resulting organizational benefits.

I was inspired to research what would happen if we went even farther in driving organizational transparency. We started small, by having the organization open its communications and processes with vendors, and it became apparent that those vendors began to compete against each other in a healthy way. From there, we explored opening the business culture with customers and employees and the entire structure and organization of a company.

The result of that research and those experiences produced the ideas and concepts I present in this book. I've been driving transformation within organizations for more than 15 years and have witnessed its positive impact on previously closed cultures that have been idle for decades. As processes mature and new information systems come in, they impact an organization. Yet most companies never change the way information is transferred to different areas. It is almost a natural evolution, especially when we look at all of the information and exchange we have that we didn't have years ago. As a result of the information now available, the culture of secrecy naturally diminishes.

Of course, transforming from a closed culture to an open one does require change. In this book, I encourage you to be receptive to possibilities and opportunities that you might not have previously entertained. Yes, it will require you to step out of your comfort zone, but so does almost any change that's worthwhile. You may need to view your company's processes from an entirely different perspective.

In the business world the numbers are stringent and the process is structured. However, creating a Culture of Open involves actively tapping your imagination and removing boundaries and limitations, so you can generate new ideas and solutions in both your work and everyday life.

Being open with and communicating with people has always been the success part of my life. Freely expressing feelings and thoughts does help in the process, especially in the business world, and it allows people to see who you are as a person, versus thinking that you have ulterior motives.

For example, one of my projects was quickly approaching deadline. Usually at those times when problems arise, people don't want to deliver bad news and, therefore, attempt to quickly fix the problem. In this instance, we were encountering significant problems. I could have chosen to let the progress continue and remain quiet about the problems. Instead, I went to the person in charge and told them they had to stop the project to avoid greater losses, even though it was a loss for me. As a result, we stopped the project. However, the client was willing to discuss the situation and eventually added funding to address it in the budget. The project drove forward and the client became part of the solution. However, if I had chosen to keep my knowledge to myself, the project would have failed and the client would have been unhappy.

The smartest organizations have been rethinking what it means to be open. This book will examine the dimensions of openness that matter most in business. We will also have a discussion on sources of openness.

Corporations once had the luxury of being closed because, quite frankly, they could be: they kept important information to themselves, especially with regard to flaws, errors, or weaknesses, and often defaulted to secrecy on a broad range of issues. Companies now operate in a hyper-transparent world: if a corporation is going to be 'naked'— and it really has no choice in the matter—it had better be in the best shape of its institutional life.

However, which corporate functions need to be involved in managing transparency? Electronics retailer Best Buy lets its customers know everything that the company knows, including data about the defect levels of the products it sells. Most customers say this is not just a matter of building trust; it is their belief that customers have a *right* to this information.

The second dimension of openness with implications for business has to do with corporate architecture and structure. The traditional, vertically integrated corporation is a paradoxical beast. Capitalist titans such as Henry Ford would champion the marketplace's virtues, yet their firms functioned like planned economies. For decades, these corporate fortresses triumphed over competitors—but no longer.

The monolithic, vertically integrated company has begun to falter against more lithe competitors. Smart companies are making their walls increasingly porous, using the Internet to open up and harness knowledge, resources, and capabilities beyond their boundaries. They establish the context for innovation, then invite their customers, partners, and other third parties to co-create their products and services. In most industries, companies can innovate and perform better by developing such networks or "business webs."

Digital technologies slash transaction and collaboration costs, and the result has been that vertically integrated corporations have been unbundling into focused business lines that work together—and are no longer siloed. The mantra "focus on what you do best and partner to do the rest" is serving leaders of the global economy well. In the past a company would outsource functions and ask for weekly or monthly status reports. As companies integrate their networks, status reports are now accessible 24/7. Rather than subcontracting processes, open companies are collaborating.

Openness contains a third dimension that can provide a competitive advantage. Today, the only meaningful assets are knowledge assets and the only meaningful capital is intellectual capital. Tesla, which has opened all of its intellectual property ("IP") to other companies, sees doing so as an advantage, rather than a disadvantage. The primary aim in doing so is growing the market in electric cars—from which Tesla can only benefit.

Conventional wisdom says you should control and protect proprietary resources and innovations—particularly intellectual property—through patents, copyrights, and trademarks. If someone infringes on your IP, get your lawyers out for battle. Many industries still think this way. Take the music industry: Tens of millions of technology-literate young people use the Internet to freely create and share MP3 software tools and music content. Digital music presents a huge opportunity to place artists and consumers at the center of a vast web of value creation. However, rather than embrace this fact and adopt new business models, the industry has taken a defensive posture and a legal response to what it views a business-model disruption. Obsession with control, piracy, and proprietary standards on the part of large industry players has only served to further alienate and anger music fans.

Today a new intellectual-property economy is prevailing. The smartest firms are treating intellectual property like a mutual fund, whereby they manage a balanced portfolio of IP assets, some protected and some shared.

Sharing IP is different from transparency. The latter is about being open and communicating pertinent information about your organization to stakeholders. Sharing is about actually giving up rights, typically to inventions, ideas, software, content, and other property. The latter is about placing property in "the commons" so that others can benefit.

For individuals and small business, this is an exciting new era—an era where they can participate in production and add value to large-scale economic systems in ways that were previously impossible. For large companies, new collaborative tools provide new ways to tap external knowledge, resources, and talent for greater competitiveness and growth. For society as a whole, we can leverage the explosion of knowledge, collaboration, and business innovation to lead richer, fuller lives and spur economic development for all.

Using the example of BP Oil and overtime, their safety record was actually worse than Exxon and other oil producers, and they worked hard to keep that information sealed, or at least unknown. Obviously, though, the truth almost always surfaces.

It doesn't matter how much effort is expended in trying to hide information—there are always people in the know. There are also the whistleblowers and the people who will bring out that information. Because of them, people run to the shredders and start shredding documents and trying to hide the information they've worked so hard not to divulge. Unfortunately, this exaggerates the problem and the problem gets bigger.

It's better to be transparent and open and get to the solution to the problem in an open capacity, versus hiding things. After all, you can almost bet that it's going to come out, regardless of the efforts made to prevent it from doing so. And when it does, the damage will be bigger.

In this book, I describe why people need to look at the fact that we live in a new world and in a digital world where the information is flowing and will go everywhere. Then I reveal how they can use that process in order to change the structure of their company and become more profitable and open to the people.

An example is the CEO of Zappos®, who decided to disclose all of the customer data that they collect out to their suppliers and anyone who was interested. Customer data is usually a gold mine for any company; therefore, they don't like to share and make their data public knowledge. But once Zappos' CEO shared that information with his customers and suppliers, revealing how much money he makes off of their products that he's trying to sell, it basically helped his suppliers react, and it helped him, as well as his customers, really understand what the profitability is and where those products are coming from. In his case, it became a success factor.

As culture of open is the future. When done with the best of intentions and toward a purpose that is beneficial to all, it has a positive impact on the organization, employees, vendors, supplies, and customers. Rather than exposing the secrets of success, it facilitates profits, accountability, and trust and becomes the major driver of innovation. The Culture of Open is an evolution, not a revolution. I invite you to explore the journey with me.

1

CULTURE OF
OPEN

"Organizations, by their very nature, are designed to promote order and routine. They are inhospitable environments for innovation."

T. Levitt

IN ORDER TO UNDERSTAND THE CULTURE OF OPEN, WE MUST first address the definition of "open." While there are different levels of openness, for our purposes, open means to be transparent. We also need to understand copyright and the difference between "Free" and "Open."

Free vs. Open: There is some confusion between the terms "free" and "open." The former should sometimes be understood with the meaning it has in "free speech" and sometimes with the meaning "free beer." The word "open" refers to the fact that the original author has not closed the source code, which can be reproduced or modified without the author's previous authorization. Thus, the popular software ADOBE® may be downloaded at no cost (contrary to other applications, such as PHOTOSHOP®), but its source code cannot be modified. It is, therefore, "free," but not "open." Open also relates to a practice where information is shared freely and without reservation—there is an environment where individuals can readily access this information and are encouraged to do so.

The *Oxford English Dictionary* defines copyright as "the exclusive legal right, given to the originator or their assignee for a fixed number of years, to publish, perform, film or record literary, artistic, or musical material, and to authorize others to do the same." Although there might be considerable differences between nations' copyright laws, especially between those practicing civil law and those adhering to common law, there is general agreement that two sets of "rights" exist: *Moral rights* give authors the right to be identified as such, and to object to derogatory treatment of their works, while *economic rights* confer an exclusive right to commercial profit for a set number of years, after which the work becomes part of the *public domain*. Legally, an author can renounce his economic rights, but cannot renounce his moral rights.

Two international bodies, *UNESCO* created in 1945, and the *World Intellectual Property Organization* (WIPO), created in 1967, have the mandate to stimulate creativity and develop collaboration between countries to harmonize their national legislations gradually. According to the WIPO, the purpose of copyright is twofold: "To encourage a dynamic creative culture, while returning value to creators so that they can lead a dignified economic existence, and to provide widespread, affordable access to content for the public."

Some international conventions already included provisions on copyright. The most important of these is certainly the *Berne Convention* of September 9, 1886, which is now ratified by 164 countries. In 1994, the *World Trade Organization* adopted an *Agreement on Trade-Related Aspects of Intellectual Property Rights*, including border measures to fight counterfeiting. The *World Intellectual Property Organization Treaty on Copyright*, signed in 1996, now protects computer programs and databases, thus adapting the *Berne Convention* to the digital age.

However, the Internet and the digital technology, while abolishing borders, have drastically disrupted this new, emerging world order. The upside to digital technology—particularly the Internet—is how quickly and widely knowledge can be diffused. The downside is the outgrowth and ease of things like illegal downloading. Thus, some photo-sharing websites reproduce millions of photos under the names of "owners" who are not the ones who took them, and millions of songs are downloaded without their rightful creators receiving a dime.

Because of the exponential multiplication of these illegal activities, national legislation on copyright is progressively becoming obsolete, since it cannot keep pace with technological progress. On the other hand, the laws that are being passé are becoming more and more complex, legal fees to have one's rights recognized by a court of justice are becoming prohibitive, and—except in rare circumstances—multinational companies are the only ones that can afford to legally go after digital offenders.

Let's define a closed culture. There are a number of ways to identify a closed culture, but the presence of any of the following features is usually a clear sign of a partially closed culture:

- **Ruled via secrecy by default:** Business information is closed and on a need-to-know basis. Typically, only the senior management team has access to all the information (e.g., salaries and bonuses, detailed financials of the organization, etc.). These multi-layered secrets often form part and parcel of the power structure: the higher you are, the more information you are able to access.

- **Has a top-down, hierarchical management:** This can be implemented with varying degrees of flexibility, but the common element is that, as an employee, you have a boss, and should do what he or she tells you. All closed cultures enable some element of push back from those who are savvy enough to know how to make their points effectively, but the general operating mode of functioning is top to bottom.

- **Structured as a pyramid—with a career ladder:** Closed organizations are without fail mapped out as pyramid shaped: there is one CEO at the top, with a "C-Suite" senior executive team below, and progressively wider layers as you go down. This pyramid also provides a career ladder—the ever-receding MacGuffin—that motivates people to work hard so they can one day get to, or near, the top of the pyramid and truly success.

- **Focuses on profit:** The more advanced closed organizations tend to focus on profit above all. This is measured as a number, and is the primary driver of decision-making. If an action results in more profit, it's worth doing. If the company makes more profit, it is more successful. Profit is the essential driver of all decisions. "How will it affect the bottom line?" is the main (or perhaps even only) question being asked.

- **Guided by motivational measurements and individual incentives:** As they mature, closed organizations begin to apply metrics as a way to ensure performance. Companies will gauge everything that can be measured and make up targets and projections (with varying degrees of involvement from those being measured), then hold people accountable to those targets. Those who meet these goals are rewarded, and those who fail are punished.

- **Encourages fixed roles and masks:** In closed cultures, as an employee, you are hired for a specific role. If you start in a non-managerial role, you can progress toward such responsibilities through promotion. Typically, doing things outside of your role is discouraged (if only because it will step on the toes of the person who currently owns that role). In closed organizations, you *are* your role. It's no surprise then that most people put on a mask to go to work: while they are at the office, they are no longer a full person with a variety of wants and activities and aspirations, but a "web developer" or a "marketing manager." Professional behavior is all that's accepted, and it's all that's given.

- **Ruled by distrust and control:** A fundamental assumption of closed cultures is that people are lazy and cannot be trusted, so they need to be controlled; otherwise, they will not do any work. This gives even more justification to adding more measurements and narrowly defining roles and performance criteria. When they don't treat them like mindless cogs in a machine, closed cultures tend to treat employees like irresponsible children.

There are countless examples of closed cultures: most of the companies and organizations in the world are run on the closed model. In fact, in many countries it is illegal to run a public company in an open way. You've most likely worked for a closed company at some point in your life. In fact, chances are you're working in one right now.

While closed cultures (which form the majority of business cultures today) are clearly capable of delivering great results, they have a number of deadly flaws, which I'll cover in more detail a later in this book. For now, let's look more closely at open cultures.

Just as there are many ways to run a closed culture, there are even more ways to run an open one. Because an open culture is, in fact, open, there really are no set rules or boundaries. This leaves the company free to mold and model their business however they please, and in a way that is best suited to the environment and climate they want to create. Each open company tends to have its own way of expressing its culture. However, these are some commonalities that are hallmarks of an open culture:

- **Creates transparency by default:** In open cultures, business information is publicly available to all employees. This includes salaries, but also bad news, strategic plans, problems, decisions, ideas, etc. People are trusted to be able to handle that information.

- **Advocates flat hierarchy and/or self-management:** If everyone knows everything and you've hired smart people in the right kinds of jobs, it is very difficult to maintain an arbitrary hierarchy, since everyone can contribute to any decision. When you trust people, it is also unnecessary to set up managers whose job it is to check after them.

- **Fosters personal development via work:** When there is no career ladder, how do people achieve career progression? The obvious solution is that they take on more responsibilities without having to go "up" an arbitrary ladder. As a natural consequence of that, it is possible for people to fully express themselves in their work by getting involved in their full range of interests, so they can achieve more personal development than they would in a narrow role with a career ladder.

- **Focuses on multiple stakeholders, values, and purpose:** In open organizations, the idea of valuing profit above all others becomes absurd. It's shareholders, employees, suppliers, customers, society, and the culture of the environment that matter. The company does not exist in a vacuum. Values become a way to express what the company cares about, rather than just a motivational slogan. Along with the higher purpose of the company, these values become the way that decisions get made in open cultures.

- **Moves away from traditional incentives:** There is a progression from the closed-culture approach of individual and team incentives toward the ultimate ideal: a system where base pay is determined by a combination of what the person is contributing, what the person needs, and what the company can afford—along with company-wide bonuses. Individual incentives are shunned.

- **Offers opportunities for self-determined pay:** One of the surefire signs of an open culture is when people determine their own pay. In most companies, this is unthinkable. In open cultures, it becomes a natural consequence of all the other factors. After all, if you trust people to make all sorts of important decisions about the company, why not trust them to make this decision, too?

- **Separates roles from people:** The idea that, as an employee, you and your role are intrinsically bound becomes patently absurd in an open culture. People are not their roles, and capable of engaging in several roles simultaneously, contributing more fully to an organization's needs. This further enables people to feel more accomplished and to be fully themselves at work, instead of wearing masks. As a result, employees are able to lend their creativity and ideas and develop and contribute a broader scope of skills that benefit the company. One of the ways this is accomplished is through open allocation.

- **Encourages trust:** Arguably the greatest strengths of open cultures is that they treat employees like adults, trusting them to do the right thing, even in complex or ambiguous situations. There are, of course, processes to help people make better decisions, but the key point is that all these processes start from a perspective of trust and responsibility.

Employees at companies with open cultures are more engaged, happier, more creative, and feel more vested in and willing to vigorously contribute to their company's bottom-line success. This also makes individuals much more fun to work with—be they founder or employee—and also far more productive. Employees work more effectively when doing so for a company they care about.

Having a better environment makes it easier to hire great people, and these people are attracted to companies that value them and their contributions.

Open cultures are far more adaptable to change. Change management is an oxymoron in an open culture: change happens constantly and continually, not through expensive, long-winded, and often failure-prone change processes.

Because they're better at motivating employees and stakeholders, open cultures often find they are also better at achieving sustainable, long-term financial results.

In the startup realm, GrantTree®, Buffer®, Valve® and Github® are examples of open cultures. Other companies include Semco®, Burtzorg®, and Happy Startup®. Many companies—regardless of size or sector—could adopt an open culture, but most don't. Why is that?

Reinventing Organisations, by Frederic Laloux, studies a dozen or so open cultures and concludes that there are two mandatory prerequisites for an open culture to exist—and be sustainable. The first is that the head of the company/ CEO and key stakeholders must be fully supportive of this (currently) unconventional way of operating.

Otherwise, when the company encounters major setbacks or challenges, the CEO and key stakeholders may feel pressure to return to a more traditional (i.e., closed) mode of business. So the obvious reason why more companies are not currently open is because most CEOs and stakeholders are not prepared to let go of a mindset of control, and when they are, the key stakeholders (whether private owners or VCs with board seats and a traditional, closed mindset, or simply public markets) frequently won't let them.

If you're the founder of a startup, this poses an interesting issue: Are you up to the challenge of creating an open culture in your business? Even when that involves giving up the trappings of power? Even when that involves passing on an investment round from an investor who you know will force the company to change its ways when it hits a rough patch?

Being open is being able to connect with people and your customers and your suppliers in in a truthful and honest way. If you're experiencing a problem, you let them know. And if you're doing well, you let them know. It must be open both ways.

From the customer perspective, if you go to Walmart and buy a T-shirt for $12, you might think that's an expensive price. However, once you've realized that it takes 10,000 gallons of water in order to create that T-shirt, and the cost to make it and bring it to market, you and other customers might be willing to pay more for it—especially if the company that's manufacturing it is more transparent in their processes, is paying a fair wage, and is being more conservative with the natural resources they're using. That's the power of open.

The other side of an open culture pertains to intellectual property and how sharing yours can enhance your IP, without enabling your competition to overrun you. Tesla®, for instance, has created a competitive advantage through IP transparency. Tesla and Elon Musk® opened up their patents, saying that others can use their patents—without fear of being sued. Their patents are currently being used by several competing car companies to enhance the features their automobiles offer.

Whether a company has a problem or is doing well, being open also means being open with the supply chain and educating the public. This is relevant for any sector, including the government. While the government doesn't directly impact the supply chain in this instance, the government is a prime example of educating the public. Insofar as WikiLeaks®, all of the things that WikiLeaks exposed around the government and what the NSA is doing cannot be hidden forever. The information is going to come out. As we've seen, much of it already has.

Looking at statistics, 80% of the intelligence that government seems very secretive about is actually on the web. People will find it. They have found it. It's already there—but the government doesn't want to tell you where to find it. The data that the secret government collects on the open web is actually more accurate than the data that they collect in other secretive ways.

Another advantage to openness: It makes both management and employees more diligent. Everyone is always trying to cross their t's and dot their i's. Everyone at the firm examines their internal processes, knowing that their division, and the organization overall, can't keep things hidden from anyone—be it customers or internal management. That level of exposure and transparency empowers stakeholders to more effectively let you know what you're doing right—and what you're doing wrong.

Authenticity is another aspect of openness—there is no room for spin or PR. Companies also have to be genuine in their desire for openness. Implementation of this desire also has to be systematic—which means it can't be a one-time event. It has to permeate the organization from top to bottom, and requires a cultural change within the organization. The process also needs to be proactive, which means that any information anticipated by persons in the process has to be proactive between customers, suppliers and employees—not reactive.

This means that an organization would have to make every attempt to inform consumers of the costs of manufacturing and delivering a product before the consumer makes the decision to purchase it—not after the consumer has decided not to purchase it because they perceived it to be too expensive. A business would opt to advise its employees, customers, and suppliers of potential problems, challenges, or obstacles before they occur—not wait to inform them after the fact. This is beneficial to the business, because it would give those segments the opportunity to weigh in, brainstorm, and actually create ideas that would circumvent or prevent these issues from arising altogether.

Shared information also has to be timely. Giving three years of back information doesn't do anyone any good. It has to be on time, in real time. And the information has to be presented in a way that people can act upon. This means that the information has to be clear and concise. It can't be a data dump, which makes it less likely that people would actually find the information they're seeking. People are not going to take the time to search that diligently. The information also has to be verifiable by a third party.

When looking at a traditional corporate viewpoint toward openness, let's use Henry Ford as an example. Ford created his own assembly line and the Model T. That whole process was very closed. Even though he had a revolutionary idea and other people started to copy it after a while, it was grounded in hierarchies and management structures. Another example is the traditional military process, with commanders on the top, followed by lower ranks, all the way down to the foot soldiers. The whole process is hierarchical, and it's a one-way process, not two-way communication. The Culture of Open requires a two-way communication process.

In two-way communication, the information flows up and down between your customers and/or employees. There has to be a feedback loop built into the process, creating a circle, versus a vertical hierarchy. A great illustration of this: In the *Knights of the Round Table,* the purpose of the round table (versus a square table) was so everyone sitting at that table would be at the same rank, and no one would be sitting at the head of that table—the prestigious seat that signifies the person of most significance.

There are many reasons why corporations opt to be closed—one of them is fear. Another is tradition: That's just how the business has been conducted for a very, very long time. "That's how it's always been done" is quite possibly the biggest creativity and innovation killer of all time.

An experiment conducted by UCLA several years ago is a good example of this: They gathered five monkeys and placed a banana at the top of a ladder. Every time a monkey would start climbing up the ladder, they would soak all of the monkeys with cold water. After a while, every time a monkey decided to go up the ladder, the other monkeys would beat him up and pull him down because they didn't want to get soaked with water.

Then they slowly started replacing the monkeys one by one, and every time a new monkey was introduced, the new monkey would go up the ladder and they would beat him up. At the end of the process, all of the five monkeys were replaced but none of them dared to go up the ladder, even though none of them had gotten wet—they had just learned from the other monkeys not to climb the ladder. Because none of them were ever soaked by water, they wouldn't have known what would happen if a monkey went up the ladder. They just did what the other monkeys had done, without really knowing why.

The bottleneck to openness has always been in the CEO and C-level offices, where access to proprietary information is a form of power. The more they can hold, the more powerful they are. But in the new digital age, that perspective is no longer viable.

A great example is Linux® versus Microsoft®. Microsoft dominated the desktop, but they eventually started falling behind. Linux is now running 90% of the servers in the world because of the openness of the Linux software. As Microsoft lost their advantage, they began to make changes and started becoming more open. However, the process appears to be reactive, not proactive, and it's true that Microsoft hasn't fully embraced the open culture concept, though they have made some progress.

What are the benefits of adopting and exhibiting an open culture? To help you understand, let's turn to Google® and Apple®. Apple has always been a very closed corporate environment, yet by all standards, it's still an extremely successful company with huge cash reserves. Conversely, look at Google and Android®, which is on an open platform. Other companies are now using it to innovate their own projects, and as a result, they're outpacing Apple in some areas. Google created Android, but by making it a free operating system, HDC®, Samsung®, and other companies have taken advantage of it. Google is reaping the benefits from that.

Apple has been plagued with a lot of issues around their iOS® system and all of their devices, largely in part because they are relying on specific individuals or roles within their company can do everything. They're finding that no one company has the capabilities or capacity to be it all and do it all. Going open source gives a company access to far more minds than they could ever afford to keep on payroll. More and more companies these days are going into a shared IP information platform. That environment, and Google is a big model of it, has enabled them to become giants.

An open culture involves more than consumers and competition. Take a look at the benefits to employees: It's important that they understand what goes on in their company. When people don't have access to accurate, credible information, rumors fly and negative thoughts run amuck. It is human nature to jump to conclusions or automatically suspect the worst, even if that is not the case. As a result, people tend to suspect there is an underlying motive when information is not fully disclosed. However, in an open culture, when people know what's going on, whether it's good, bad or indifferent, they're aware of what's happening in real time, and can make better-informed decisions that help the company grow and innovate.

When employees feel valued and are happy, they also contribute more, are more productive, and less likely to seek new employment.

When an employee joins a company and stays with the company for a significant period of time, that employee becomes an investment through the cost of recruitment, training, and benefits. When a company loses an employee, that's a living piece of brain trust that walks out the door.

It will take time, expense, and effort for a new employee to have as much value as an experienced one. And, depending on the employee and his or her contributions, skills, and talents, some of the value of a lost employee may never be fully recouped or regained by the business. Happier employees means loyal employees, which translates to longer-term employment—and good fiscal policy.

Transparency and openness is also important in innovation. For example, Google tells all of their employees that they should spend 20% of their time working on a project that they like that has nothing to do with their jobs and what they do. That has helped Google grow, because a number of different products that come out of Google actually started at someone's desk as he or she thought it was a cool idea to explore. If the project was worthwhile, Google invested money behind it. This makes employees feel empowered, and that they not only can make a difference, but have a direct impact on their company's bottom line. As you can see, this transparency and openness only works when it is two ways—first, Google provides the open environment where employees are free to dedicate 20% of their working time toward a personal idea. On the flip side, the employee must also be open and willing to share the projects that they're working on with Google.

The impact of openness on a company's relationship with its vendors and partners is that if supply chain data is transparent and all stakeholders have access to who your customers are, what they want, what they're buying, and their patterns, your suppliers can react much more quickly in order fulfilment. If vendors and partners know, for example, that a company's customers have a high consumer demand for red shoes, they can make sure they have supplies in that color. If your suppliers don't have access to this information, are focused solely on the manufacturing side of the supply chain, and don't have any direct interaction with customers or access to relevant data, there will be shortfalls and back orders. If that information flows freely between a company, its suppliers, and its customers, it becomes a more fluid process. This transparency enables companies to anticipate and produce more of the specific items their customers want—rather than focusing on what their customers might want, and missing the mark. Again, it's becoming proactive—rather than reactive. It's always better to supply customers with what they want, rather than scrambling to meet unmet demands. If the supply isn't there when demand is, customers will turn elsewhere for their products.

Consumers and customers are observant. They pay attention and understand the difference between Company A and Company B. When they have a choice, they usually look for the responsible company. What does this mean? It means that while consumers are cognizant of price and quality, they actually consider themselves to be in a relationship with the company. In that relationship they made decisions about whether they like or dislike a company's practices and agree or disagree with their policies. In most instances, they will prefer to engage in a business relationship with a company that is socially and environmentally responsible.

If Company A is open and transparent about their labor practices, their supply chain processes, and where they get their product, it can make a difference to a customer. Some companies will choose Company A over Company B because they have no idea how Company B's products are sourced. Years ago, Walmart® started their "made in America" platform, which appealed to their customers. In doing so, Walmart profited by opening up a certain piece of their supply chain and informing their customers which of their products are American-made.

Walmart's "made in America" platform jumped Walmart's sales numbers because consumers thought they were getting an American-made product, versus one manufactured in China. This distinction made a big difference to some of their customers (a *Consumer Reports* survey revealed that 80 percent of Walmart's American shoppers preferred to buy products made in the U.S.). Not surprising, the sluggish economy in 2013 played a role in consumer preferences and the launch of Walmart's program. Some consumers like to know that their money is supporting businesses and people in their own communities and countries.

Consumers are becoming more conscious about what they're buying, what they're eating, and what they're doing in their everyday life—and this level of transparency helps consumers to make better decisions.

In 2014, Microsoft opened up their .NET development tool packages for anyone to view and improve upon it. Microsoft is moving into the world of openness right now because they realized that they were falling behind by holding all their cards so closely to their proverbial chest.

Sharing patent details is another recent trend in openness.

Google strives to maintain the open culture often associated with startups, in which everyone is a hands-on contributor and feels comfortable sharing ideas and opinions. In its weekly all-hands ("TGIF") meetings—not to mention exchanges over email or in its company cafeterias—Googlers ask questions directly to Larry Page and Sergey Brin, and other Google executives about any company issue. Their offices and cafeterias are designed to encourage interactions between Googlers within and across teams, and to spark conversation about work, as well as play.

In 1885, George Selden from Rochester, New York was granted US Patent 549, which gave him exclusive rights to a two-cycle gasoline engine. This slowed down, rather than boosting, the development of the car manufacturing industry in the United States. In 1911, Henry Ford, an independent automaker, challenged this patent and won. This led to the creation of the *Motor Vehicle Manufacturers Association* and a cross-licensing agreement among all US auto manufacturers: although each company would develop technology and file patents, these patents were shared openly without the exchange of money.

The same concept of sharing and progress based on everybody's work is at the base of open culture in computing. In the early days, computers were sold with open software. Gradually, most software companies decided to close their source code, making it impossible to alter their products. To demonstrate his disagreement, Richard Stallman, who was working with the Massachusetts

Institute of Technology, resigned in February of 1984 and launched the GNU project. In 1989, he created the General Public License, which gave interested researchers not only the ability to have access to the source code, but also to reproduce, modify, and distribute it.

Soon, however, the movement split in two different directions. Stallman and the Free Software Foundation, created in 1985, adopted a social dimension by putting the emphasis on knowledge sharing, while Éric Raymond and his Open Source Initiative (OSI), which was created in 1998, stressed the possibilities for technological development opened up by the fact that developers could freely use their predecessors' work.

On the Internet, Wikipedia® came on line in January, 2001. This electronic encyclopedia is probably the most commonly known and used example of information sharing. It now offers 16 million articles in 270 languages and attracts 78 million visitors.

Flickr® is a photo-sharing site, launched in 2004 by Ludicorp of Vancouver and acquired subsequently by Yahoo®. In September of 2010, it contained more than five billion photos.

While there has been some awareness into the need to be more transparent and open, there are still organizations that thrive on secrecy. The US government is one. For instance, the US government went to great lengths to maintain secrecy about the data behind weapons of mass destruction in Iraq. That was big, and one reason there was such a huge cloak of secrecy surrounding it was because they hadn't verified their information and, unfortunately, much of the information couldn't be verified at all. And all of that secrecy around it, good, bad, or indifferent, became a problem for the US government when they attempted to move forward with it.

Another example is the BP Oil® disaster, which brought out some questionable safety practices. If they were transparent and open, all of the negativity, public outcry, and subsequent fall out could have been prevented.

BP Oil, the U.S. government, and many other businesses who have been subjected to negative judgment due to their reluctance to disclose information could have benefited from adopting an open culture. Being open is being free from pretense and deceit and characterized vividly by making information accessible. In order for this to occur, though, the environment has to change at the top—the company's leader(s) need to implement policies and practices that lend themselves to an open culture as it pertains to the public and their employees.

Great leaders know they need to cultivate the skills of their workforce, while simultaneously building a work environment that motivates, excites, and inspires their employees. Not surprisingly, companies that are committed to developing a strong workplace culture tend to perform well.

However, building this type of environment takes sustained time, effort, and resources. Some organizations will adeptly catalyze the successes of employees—and others will not.

For over a century, corporations have ruled with a top-down mentality. Management experts have long encouraged businesses to set objectives and targets that map to well-defined priorities and plans.

But those standards are evolving. Today's new benchmark of success is not only to execute with excellence, but to do so while managing rapid change.

The rising forces of globalization and technology over the past decade have inherently changed the way we communicate, exchange information, and work. Working in today's economy means operating in a 24/7 digital environment, across various time zones and cultures across the globe.

Taking note of the popularity of social sharing, organizations are now looking at adopting new models of working that tap into the collective intelligence of an organization's networks. To do this, CEOs are showing a growing appetite for technology—specifically social media technology—to infuse more collaboration into everyday business functions.

As CEOs ratchet up the level of openness within their organizations, they are developing collaborative environments where employees are encouraged to speak up, exercise personal initiative, connect with fellow collaborators, and innovate. But at the same time, CEOs are reinforcing the strength of their corporate character. In order to manage the risks associated with an open workplace, an organization's values must be responsibly practiced and upheld. Employees will willingly engage as an organization's brand ambassadors if they are appropriately guided and empowered.

From both inside and out, these leaders are encouraging employees, clients, and partners to connect and learn from each other. According to a 2012 IBM® CEO study, more than half of CEOs (53 percent) are planning to use technology to facilitate greater partnering and collaboration with outside organizations, while 52 percent are shifting their attention to promoting great internal collaboration.

According to the study, additional strategies that CEOs hope to implement to revitalize the strength of their organizations include:

- **Developing flexible employees:** To build its next-generation workforce, organizations have to actively recruit and train employees who excel at working in open, team-based environments. At the same time, leaders must build and support practices to help both new and existing employees thrive, such as encouraging the development of unconventional teams, promoting experiential learning techniques, and facilitating the use of high-value employee networks.

- **Strengthening employees through company values**: For CEOs, organizational openness offers tremendous upside potential, including empowered employees, free-flowing ideas, more creativity and innovation, happier customers, and better results. However, greater openness also comes with more risk. As rigid controls loosen, organizations need a strong sense of purpose and shared beliefs to guide decision making. Employees must truly believe in the purpose, mission, and values of the organization. And to develop a shared belief system, employees must help create it.

- **Leading by example:** Championing collaborative innovation is not something CEOs are delegating to their HR leaders. According to the study's findings, the business executives surveyed are interested in leading by example. While social media is still an uncharted frontier for many, business leaders understand the power of technology to facilitate valuable connections. Like their employees, CEOs must reinvent themselves and invest the time to build new skills and familiarize themselves with new tools.

Building a great workplace is not something that will happen overnight. However, this transformation can be achieved if an organization makes a long-term investment in its people and puts the right tools and processes in place to help them succeed.

Forward-looking business leaders understand that the new connected era is fundamentally changing how people engage with the organization and each other. These changes are putting new pressures on organizations to adapt, but they are also creating new opportunities to innovate and lead.

2

CULTURE OF
INNOVATION

*"When you're trying to create things that are new, you
have to be prepared to be on the edge of risk."*

Michael Eisner

AN OPEN ORGANIZATION IS A HEALTHY BREEDING GROUND FOR
innovation.

Innovation is critical to spark growth, and trust sparks
innovation! High-trust companies are innovative in the
products and services they offer customers, and they have
strong cultures of innovation, which only thrive in an
environment of high trust.

High trust levels make your career and your organization
thrive. When trust is high, the dividend received is like a
performance multiplier, elevating and improving
innovation and growth in every dimension of your
organization. Innovation and creativity demand a number
of important conditions to flourish, including information
sharing, an absence of caring about who gets the credit, a
willingness to take risks, the safety to make mistakes, and

the ability to collaborate. And all of these conditions are the fruits of high trust.

The benefits of innovation are clear: opportunity, revenue growth, and market share. Apple Computer—nearly "dead" at one time—first rejuvenated itself through innovation in the development of the iPod® and the iTunes® Music Store. Recently, *Business Week* and *The Boston Consulting Group* ranked Apple as the most innovative company in the world. It was a remarkable transformation in a remarkably short period of time.

As John Marchica notes in *The Accountable Organization*: "Many heralded Apple's service as a savior of the music industry ... With the introduction of iTunes, it appeared that ... [Apple CEO Steve] Jobs ... finally got it right. Consumers don't want to be treated like criminals, and artists don't want their valuable work stolen," he remarked. "The iTunes Music Store offers a ground-breaking solution for both."

High trust increases value in two dimensions: shareholder value and customer value. High-trust organizations consistently innovate and deliver more value to their customers. We see this with every new release of the iPhone, another Apple product that has a loyal consumer base that continuously looks forward to the newest version and the new features it offers.

When we look at the research and development process and openness, Linux is one of the best examples. Linux went through a major innovation cycle and has become dominant in the server world because of the power that *wasn't* behind it. When Linus Torvalds created Linux, he just put the kernel out there and said, "Here's something I've created. See how you guys can improve upon it."

It took off from there, and hundreds and thousands of people started working on it on their own time. If he had decided to make this a closed-source process, he never would have been able to improve the Linux kernel to the point that it is today. And he never would have benefited from the subsequent innovations.

Innovative workers are attracted to an organization with a reputation for innovation. In the information technology market specifically, there are many people who want to work for Google. Why not Microsoft? Microsoft traditionally has been a very closed process and had been until 2014 when they got a new CEO. Prior to that, their practices were very old, traditional, and structured. There is no comparison to Google, where hierarchy is basically non-existent. It was their openness that helped Google become powerful. They started as a search engine company, but now they're dominating phones, building driverless cars, running networks, and expanding their products and services beyond what anyone would have ever envisioned.

The people in a company respond to its culture, and it's the culture of the company that drives innovation into that process. Insofar as Google and Microsoft, most of their partners would prefer to work with Google. The only reason they work with Microsoft is because Windows® has been traditionally dominant in the market, and as a result, they can't afford not to work with Microsoft. But as soon as Google announces something new, everybody jumps on that bandwagon, profitable or not, because they know that there are a lot of innovators behind it who are going to make it successful.

Openness within an organization encourages innovators. When information is flowing in an organization and people know what other colleagues are working on and are free to add to that innovation, they can jump in and help to drive it. It creates a culture of cooperation that helps to break down the walls and barriers between people and titles.

In companies like Microsoft, somebody always had to be at the bottom. Instead of people running faster to get ahead of everybody else, they figured if they trip the other person and the other person falls, they wouldn't have to run as fast. The culture created defensiveness and competition within the company, rather that cooperation toward mutual ideas, innovation, and progress. On the other hand, we have Google, which is an open culture, where people are not afraid of sharing ideas and sharing information with each other. As a whole, the entire organization operates in that process.

In a closed environment, it's not unusual for employees to do what is expected of them and nothing more. They have job duties and responsibilities, and only have permission to work on those specific things. Because of this, there is no incentive, or even permission, for them to contribute in other ways, adding their ideas, knowledge, or opinions to current or future projects. Even if they did have something to contribute, it's unlikely that they would be aware of new ideas in order to do so.

In an open environment, in an open culture, ideas are being exchanged all of the time. All the information is available to everybody all of the time. People actually want to get involved. And people who you would never suspect might have an idea that can help drive the company into a new direction step up. It's all about information being available and people knowing that their ideas are welcome into the process.

An open organization rewards its innovators. If we look at traditional companies, they have two elements of growth— what I call horizontal growth and vertical growth.

Horizontal growth is opening up new markets, finding new customers and new people, and becoming more global. A vertical process, however, is where we can see a real difference. It's coming out with new ideas and new products into the market.

Most traditional American companies are on a horizontal path. They're basically selling the same things, and doing the same things, they've always sold and done, just in a different market in a different place in a different format. It's not a breeding ground for innovation. Innovation comes out of the vertical process. It is giving your employees the space, time, and resources to create. The company shares their desire for a breakthrough culture with their employees. They don't just want to sell the same thing over and over again in new places. At a certain point, it will become apparent that there are only so many places on earth where they can keep going and selling the same thing. Eventually, they'll reach the limit on geographic expansion.

That was BlackBerry's® downfall. They had a very successful business model and started to expand it into different markets, especially consumer markets. When they got to the consumer, it became apparent that what was good for the business wasn't really good for the consumer. And to put the final nail in their coffin, they failed to innovate beyond their original product. They were selling the same thing and thinking that selling the same thing in a new market would help, but it didn't. Everybody else went flying by them, and they are in the position they are today because of that mistake.

An open organization is a group that is more driven by the collective, versus individual. Everybody contributes, and no one person becomes a hero in the process. Traditionally, in Western cultures, we're all about heroes and having one person basically carrying the flag and being the beacon in driving that process. It's the cult of personality. In industries that revolve around innovation, however, that can lend to a cut-throat environment that impedes progress and innovation, rather than feeding it.

In an open organization, the team wins as a whole. One person might come up with an ingenious idea at the beginning, but it's not about that one person in the end because it takes a life of its own. As everybody contributes a little to it, it becomes bigger and bigger. And as often happens in an open organization, the end result is an idea that is a significantly improved version of the original concept—and all because many people had the ability to conceptualize, create, and contribute to the end product.

Here's a fictional example of how it would work in a company that designs and creates manufactured homes. An architect illustrates the layout and exterior design of a three-bedroom, two-story home with energy saving features. All of the employees, including the CEO, the interior designers, plumbers, electricians, carpenters, roofers, etc. have access to the new design. An interior designer takes a look and sees something with promise, but finding it rather cold and drab, plays with the exterior, finding materials and colors that are appealing and more energy efficient. The electrician steps in and proposes a solar and wind energy system that would make the house totally reliant on nature.

The carpenters get in on the excitement and propose framing the house out of existing steel shipping structures that are no longer being used, instead of boards—thus making the house stronger and safer, the structure more fire resistant, all while saving trees and repurposing items in an environmentally friendly manner. The plumbers suggest creating a water saving system by capturing rainwater.

Then the builders go to work, creating a process that allows the home to be built off site and assembled on site in record time.

Every person on board contributes another idea. In the end, rather than having one more traditional house to add to a consumer's list of choices, they have created an entirely new product that appeals to a broader market. One idea generated another, until the company found itself in a position to be at the forefront in the creation and development of manufactured homes with energy efficiency. It's not a far stretch to see that this process could lend itself to any company's expansion beyond their original product, as its employees create and improve on existing features to make an offering more useful and desirable to a broadened consumer market.

In this example, does the architect get the credit because she was the one who first designed the home? Absolutely not, because the house was designed by employees across the entire company, and each one contributed toward the final product.

That's how it was in the world of Linux. Linus Torvalds was the guy who created the Linux kernel at the beginning. But Linux is not defined by him. A whole community of people contributed to it and made it what it is today. You can't say that one person created that whole process. It's more about community effort and the whole process of thousands and thousands of developers each contributing to what Linux is today.

In order to nurture an innovative culture within an organization, there must be information, open resources, and communication. People need to be able to filter that communication and react to it. It requires transparency and two-way communication touching everyone in the organization. An open organization believes that innovators can be found anywhere, and that everybody has a good idea that can contribute to a process.

What does a culture of innovation look like? It is structured in circles, and the circles are empowered to drive that innovation process. There is no hierarchy in the process. There's a democratic process within those circles. Look at the Internet today with all of its communities—bloggers, Facebook, Twitter, Google+, etc.—there is no one person in charge of that structure. It's basically an amalgamation of everybody coming into a common place.

An open organization structure is basically a radical shift from what we know today—which is a hierarchical process. It's a circular process where everybody is part of a project and a team, and whether that team wins or loses, they do it as a team. In that team, there is no real structured format or formal process. I describe it as managed chaos. In order to be innovative, you have to break down the boxes that people put themselves in. We've all heard the term "think outside of the box." My thinking is, why does there even have to be a box? In the Linux example I cited earlier, there is really no structure, no format, and no quotas. It's a process of people getting together and interacting over ideas.

However, that chaos does have to be managed, which is why processes are put in place. There has to be someone or some group that maintains and drives things in a certain direction and from a certain perspective. But people are able to branch out of that structure as well. For example, if you start with one circle, it might evolve into three circles, each with a different focus. Then they merge back into one circle, and at a certain point, it branches back out into two circles. The managed part keeps it moving in the same direction so they don't lose the elasticity that comes with the process and brings them back into the same circle.

Communication is one thing that does not have to be managed. The information should be there whenever it's needed. It's a matter of enabling the organization to have readily available data for whoever wants it, however they want it, and in whatever format they need it. This process shouldn't necessitate paperwork, approval, or multiple steps. It's enabling a structure within the organization so people can freely get the information they need, in the format and structure that works best for them. It can be as simple as accessing group files stored on a company's server.

To allow communication of innovative ideas, you first need to understand the goals and direction of a company. That knowledge is bedrock—everything else is open. Becoming a company that creates phones was not part of Google's original business plan. But somebody came up with an idea and said, *Hey, here is a different way.* Google's business model is advertising driven. So, the big concept of "we want to sell more advertising, and that's where our revenue comes from" is the big monolithic goal that sits up front, even as it innovates in new directions.

Now, open up your company culture and if a problem needs to be solved, ask "What are the different ways we can do that?" In a traditional search engine company, people would think, "In order for us to sell advertising by going down the horizontal path, we are going to open up the Chinese and Japanese markets." This is good, but then somebody comes up with an idea and says, "Hey, if we have a smartphone that has a Google search engine as a default in it, people would go to that and use our search engine, versus using our competitors."

That innovation helped Google become the dominant operating system for smartphones. But there's more. Then somebody else said, "Well, if we have a translator as part of our Google search engine, people will come to us and look at translations of different things." Google is driving people to the services they have to offer and creating different avenues for consumer engagement. Google innovated that process. There was never really a set goal that provided a blueprint on how they were going to do that. They provided their employees with the freedom to figure out how to get to the place where Google wanted to be—through innovation and profitability drivers.

Building a community around an idea is not a conscious effort. It's a process. A company's C-suite must leave its culture open enough to foster communication and ideas and for those ideas to take flight and become different things within the organization. In an open culture you don't put someone in charge and say, "Okay, your job is to go create X and create a community around it." It's having employees who feel that they can be creative and expressive and that their ideas count and are valued. This is what Google is doing by telling their employees to use 20% of their time to do whatever they want to do. That policy never set out to create Android, but instead to foster an environment that enabled Android to be created.

Google is just one example. Other innovative companies include Tesla, Uber®, Netflix®, Steam®, Sales Force®, and Arden Mills®. On the opposite side of the spectrum are companies that lack a successful innovative culture. One example is Sony's® e-reader project. Sony's culture is hierarchical and based on a traditional process.

Netflix's original goal was to deliver movies to people. They started with the "rent a DVD and we'll send it to you and you never have to pay a late fee" concept. When that model was going away, another concept was introduced: "What if we stream the videos to the people's homes?" Netflix's goal had been to deliver movies—but they never circumscribed to their employees *how* the films should be delivered. This continual innovation keeps them relevant.

The structure of innovation is about setting a goal—a big goal upfront—and letting people creatively reach that goal without dictating the processes. In the 80s, Sony created the idea of the Walkman, which was very innovative. But the fact that they were going to build a Walkman was a focused, structured effort. Then Apple came up with the iPod and walked all over them.

Sony also came up with the first e-reader. But they couldn't get it off the ground because their structure was so enclosed. They wanted to have an e-reader, but never went out to their suppliers or worked with the community to create an e-reader the way Amazon® has. The reason Amazon came up with the e-reader wasn't that they wanted to build one; it was that they wanted to sell books, versus wanting to sell e-readers.

What is the difference between the two companies? Amazon started as a book company. Their goal was to sell books. They knew that consumers were looking for books, and they wanted different ways of getting that book into the consumer's hands. Sony is more of a hardware company, and they really focused around an e-reader. Well, an e-reader without the book doesn't really mean anything. An e-reader is nothing without content on it. Amazon wanted to serve its customers and found an ingenious way to do so.

Today's consumer market is all about information and ways of getting information to people. Google's success stems from the fact that they're delivering information. They're not delivering widgets. Sony's focus has always been around delivering widgets. And those widgets falter because not all of our devices are smart devices and everything needs to have content that goes with it. If you don't have the content with the process, then you lose.

Look at Sony's music division. Sony's music division had all kinds of issues and problems because they couldn't innovate around the content—they were trying to innovate around a widget. And that widget gets outdated pretty quickly.

Microsoft is another great example. Microsoft's human resources policies have been a complete impediment in their innovation process. Somebody comes up with an idea, and they tell their programmers to make it happen—without any revisions or alterations to the original concept. As I've mentioned before, there's always somebody at the top and there's always somebody at the bottom, and everybody else is in the middle. If you didn't want to be at the bottom, you quickly understand that you have to run faster to move up. But people quickly figured out that if they trip other people, they can get them out of the way and get to the top. It became a destructive culture within Microsoft, and people started holding information to their chest and not sharing that information and sabotaging each other. Ultimately, it stifled innovation and became Microsoft's downfall.

Changing that culture into a more open culture is really helping Microsoft. By taking away the whole hierarchical process and the measurements and statistics around how people perform, they let them be who they are and do what they do best. They have some brilliant people at Microsoft, and they do a lot of good things. They are finally allowing their team to do what they do best and do it well by embracing a more open culture.

Let's look at Google's Nine Principles of Innovation as it relates to openness:

Innovation comes from anywhere: At Google, innovation is not the purview of a specific department or elite cadre of individuals. Rather, it is everyone's responsibility. Employees are encouraged to seek innovative solutions to all immediate problems, and offer their application for other issues confronting the firm. This generates a corporate-centric brand of internal (intranet) open-sourcing unique to Google.

Focus on the user: Customer-centric product design is advocated over pure-profit motivation. Building products that are easier for customers to operate stimulates profit through customer appreciation of useful product experiences, self-advertising the item. Anything that improves the user experience brings them back to Google's website and products, generating further interest and sales, while lowering the firm's operating and advertising costs.

Think 10X, not 10%: Aim to provide a solution that is 10 times, rather than 10%, better than what currently exists. Seek radical, rather than incremental, improvement and development. Accept evidence from unlikely sources to generate unexpected, but highly practical, solutions.

Bet on technical insights: Trust state-of-the-art technology to provide at least rudimentary guidelines for new or unresolved projects and products. Information and processes used to innovate are not subject to dogmatic or doctrinal motivations. They exist beyond human influence or error and can be applied objectively. Internal, intranet open-sourcing fostering collaboration within the organization is especially open to exchange of technical insights across projects aligned with Google's strategic imperatives.

Ship and iterate: Realize that, however useful it can be, innovation never means perfection. The necessary objective of innovation is improvement. New or improved products will reach customers, who'll have their own opinions about the objects' functionality. Seek and use customer feedback about what's not perfect in the item, and redeploy, enhancing the product's quality once more with further development. Indeed, according to the essential precepts of innovation, changes will need to be made; that's the basic premise of innovation.

20% time: Google has long relied on a "20% time" philosophy, wherein all employees were allotted 20% of their work-time, about a-day-a-week, to develop and perfect side-projects. Doing so transforms all workers into innovation agents simply by following ideas they are passionate about. This 20% time exercise has resulted in the development of many of Google's successful products, such as Google News®, Google Alerts®, Gmail®, GoogleEarth®, Gmail® labs and off-road Google Maps Street View®. However, in late 2013, 20% time was re-evaluated according to deep analytics of employee performance. The idea of "focused free-thinking" remains essential to the firm's innovation culture, but in a somewhat modified form, with more attention being paid to ideas that have a clear association with Google's strategic imperatives. Nevertheless, the objective of employees sharing ideas about things they were not hired to do shows Google still values the concept of the 80-20 split; its approach has just been a bit more refined to focus on strategic initiatives. Everyone in the organization is thus given the time to authentically respond to their innovative spirit. Another way to look at this concept is intrapreneurship—essentially, entrepreneurship internally within a company. Let your employees take on side jobs and work cross-functionally with other teams.

Default to open: This principle expands Google's internal collaboration to permit a greater degree of open-sourced partnership than had previously existed. Innovation often stems from interaction of the best minds, but in a world of 7 billion people, comparatively few of them are directly employed by Google. Open-sourcing invites contributions from a far larger number of potential innovators than are normally available to the firm, bringing an international collective of minds to bear on projects of all kinds.

Fail well: Failure is a byproduct of innovation, and is frequently the source of process improvement. Ideas may not work out as planned, but they can lead to something else of value. Even if a venture is an outright failure, one can inevitably find among the ruins the remnants of good ideas that, retooled and reprocessed, can lead to future success. This "morphing" of the best aspects of a failed project frequently generates beneficial redeployment of seemingly useless projects.

Have a mission that matters: This is, perhaps, the most important of them all. An underlying theme of innovative processes, and the principles guiding them, brings corporate objectives and strategies to life. Google's products and services impact millions of people worldwide every day, which gives the firm's innovation culture a prevailing sense of useful enterprise, one based on improving communication among people, businesses, and nations. Google's mission of generating information for anyone with access to a computer—whether it be the most arcane fact about an obscure point in history or finding a living person lost during the course of a tsunami—motivates its employees to innovate globally, across all fields and disciplines, for an exceptional range of products and services.

Google's innovation culture reflects its commitment to operational excellence, steady performance, and perpetual growth, encouraging useful global collaboration and good will.

The Benefits of an Open Culture for Innovation

The Culture of Open is one that allows the best of crowdsourcing, to build a foundation for further customization.

We have seen that open standards will triumph over proprietary approaches because history tells us that where there's openness and collaboration without fear of vendor or ecosystem lock-in, business challenges are addressed and innovation thrives.

Whether it's the latest and greatest Android app built on Linux or a cloud computing solution that allows a client to work across multiple vendors, open standards mean the market can come to bear and businesses can focus on delivering value without the burden of proprietary constraints.

Open standards act as a blueprint or insurance policy that allow a variety of industries, such as healthcare, financial services, automotive, retail, energy and others, to link up and share information faster, easier, and at lower costs. That's true cross-industry collaboration and the power of interoperability—providing businesses choices and the ability to deliver better goods, services, and intelligent data that a closed, proprietary approach can't offer.

This access to global resources is only heightened as Moore's Law (a golden rule applied to computer processors, stating that the number of transistors on an integrated circuit doubles every two years) continues to prove true and we see the performance of information technologies increase while cost declines. We're finding that powerful technologies, combined with open standards and the Internet, are building a global infrastructure that provides limitless computing resources, but more important, opportunities for knowledge sharing and cooperation.

The result is a business environment where industry lines are blurred, and instead enterprises are characterized by the collaborative innovation they're able to drive based on open standards. As the foundation that allows industries to link disparate systems together faster, easier, and at lower costs, open standards are driving a variety of new solutions that will benefit industries and end users alike.

Now we see a new technology come to the crossroads to face the historical divide of proprietary vs. open. Cloud computing has the promise to transform our lives and business, just as the Web and Linux has. However, a proprietary approach can slow the economic advance of one of the most promising areas of computing.

By leading a worldwide effort to accelerate open standards in and across industries, and in new technologies such as cloud computing, we hope to propel business forward. When we're not limited to silos of a few, and can instead tap the wisdom of many. We also avoid the pitfalls of proprietary, closed systems and enjoy the benefits of open collaboration as we strive to satisfy the global demand for innovation.

Open innovation takes a company beyond its own R&D capabilities. Through this strategy, a company reaches out to access innovation resources that expand internal capabilities and become an asset for the company.

An open-outcome strategy focuses on outcomes, rather than on sources.

Here are 10 steps that companies should follow to create and cultivate a successful shift to open-innovation:

1. **Create a needs list:** This is a process that should involve senior innovation leadership, research, and product-development leaders, as well as people from the business units.

   Together create a prioritized list of critical strategic and business needs that can benefit from open-source innovation.

2. **Define the company's core competencies.** What knowledge, expertise, and technology are unique to your organization? In what areas do you lead your industry (and in what areas do you lag)?

   Knowing these answers makes it easier to be honest about where you don't have expertise and, therefore, can benefit from external innovation.

3. **Initiate scouting.** The fastest way to realize impact from open innovation is to scout for new partners and technologies against the identified needs.

   This can be through a formal request-for-proposals (RFP) process, or through more informal outreach. Build a scouting team to lead the effort, and identify experts and potential development partners who can help with ideation.

   Remember that messaging in the RFP requires great care and precision; it's important to "get to the root" of your challenge to find the best partners, who may be from unrelated industries.

   Innovation partners can be particularly helpful with this messaging process.

4. **Develop an intellectual-property strategy.** Companies' standard policies related to intellectual property need to be modified to encourage open innovation.

   Develop a strategy that facilitates the open discussions and collaboration that will enable your company to move forward and collaborate with outsiders.

   At the same time, your policies must describe upfront, and in a clear way, "who owns what."

5. **Broaden outreach to additional stakeholders**. For instance, many companies actively engage customers to identify and define their next products (such as Hallmark Cards'® use of contests to enable consumers to create new greeting cards). Others leverage their internal "brain trust" to tap into knowledge and expertise that may be hidden across the organization.

   For example, AkzoNobel®, a Netherlands-based Global 500 leader in coatings and specialty chemicals, developed a company-wide networked innovation program to help drive strategic innovation across its business units. By issuing internal, cross-business searches, they are able to uncover new solutions and pools of talent not previously considered.

6. **Let everyone know that the company is "open" to innovation**. Keep every suggestion on the table, both from internal and external sources. Being open to any idea from any source can pay off in surprising ways.

   Examples of open-innovation portals to encourage new partnerships with external technology providers abound, from companies in food and beverage (Innovate with Kraft®), consumer products (Unilever's® Working with Us), and automotive (Johnson Controls®).

7. **Transform existing relationships**. Turn the tables on conventional thinking and engage your suppliers and vendors, elevating them to strategic partners. Put agreements in place that guarantee confidentiality in the open exchange of ideas and be open to sharing long-term goals.

   Your suppliers are on the front lines of where their industry is headed. Move discussions out of the back room and work on building more strategic, trusted relationships.

8. **Build a knowledge base**. This happens typically in year two of a company's push to open innovation, and shows why it is a long-term process. You can't do this at the beginning.

    Create a repository of best practices, and see what kind of metrics you can develop to measure progress. Create mentors in the organization based on who has been able to achieve a track record of success. This is part of transforming the corporate culture that simply takes time and requires experience.

9. **Collaborate with peer organizations**. Be the company that articulates the big challenges facing your industry, and be willing to take a leadership role in addressing them.

    Executed correctly, this is an opportunity to work with competitors and deal with industry-wide issues like regulation, safety, and sustainability.

10. **Create accountability.** This should be a positive, incentivizing part of the program. Celebrate and showcase successful outcomes from collaborative innovation projects. Highlight them as big things, and celebrate individual and team achievements.

    You need to demonstrate that the company highly values this collaboration, both internally and externally.

Open innovation does not entail the creation of a massive business concept. Instead, it is the transformation of an internal culture and the development of a process to encourage and promote innovation from every available source.

As such, it is within the reach of any company—large or small—willing to make the commitment to work at it and join the ranks of innovative companies leading in today's global marketplace.

In the past few years, Cisco®, Coca-Cola®, GE®, IBM®, MasterCard® and other large companies have begun to launch "internal startups"—teams of employees who are sheltered from corporate rules and bureaucracy—to stimulate entrepreneurship and creativity, and infuse agility.

The thinking in such companies was that employees within this quasi-startup would be free to focus on their goals. Team spirit and collaboration would replace hierarchy. Innovation, risk-taking, and learning from failure would flourish. Time formerly spent on meetings and emails with other corporate groups would be spent focusing on the customer.

All those good things came true, as long as the team was left alone.

Before too long, however, someone at headquarters got the idea that the group would be more efficient if brought into the corporate fold.

The team was moved from a remote location to headquarters. The business leader, who had been sitting side-by-side with his team, trading ideas multiple times per day, moved to the "executive floor," where he could be closer to other executive leaders.

His employees stopped calling him AJ and started calling him Mr. Johnson. He traded his jeans and polo shirt for a suit, in keeping with headquarters' attire.

The easy efficiency with which he had formerly conversed with employees ended. Instead of walking to his desk to ask a question or offer an idea, they worked through his assistant to schedule a meeting or conference call with him. His schedule rapidly filled with meetings with executive peers, so subordinates often had to wait two weeks to speak with him. Five-minute conversations became thirty-minute appointments.

Relationships with suppliers changed, as well. When the team operated autonomously, suppliers were treated as partners. They were paid fairly, and they jumped through hoops to help. After being absorbed into the corporate structure, the team had to hand procurement over to specialists, who forced suppliers through an arduous bidding process. The best suppliers opted out, and the suppliers who remained existed on razor thin margins that left no room for innovation.

When autonomous, the team had achieved remarkable sales growth, driven by an extraordinary level of energy, esprit de corps and commitment to customer satisfaction. Once the team was absorbed into the corporate office, however, things slowed down, and sales growth stalled (perhaps predictably, this lower level of sales growth was accepted without protest from above—in the corporate climate, as long as sales were incrementally better than the prior year, all was well).

The former attitude of "let's do something amazing together" shifted to "let's keep our heads down and stay out of trouble."

3

CULTURE OF
RESPONSIBILITY

*"Rank does not confer privilege or give power.
It imposes responsibility."*

Peter Drucker

TRANSPARENCY AND OPENNESS WITHIN AN ORGANIZATION
doesn't just require responsibility, it also enhances
responsibility. In my opinion, there are different levels of
responsibility—including responsibility to your customers,
employees, suppliers, the environment, and humanity as a
whole. Openness helps a company be transparent in the
process in the process of dealing with the aforementioned
groups.

A Culture of Responsibility includes educating customers
about what a responsible company does and how that
responsibility translates to prices and its sourcing of
materials. Openness will help in the process of becoming a
more responsible company because, as I once heard
someone say, "When you get naked, you can't be fat." Being
naked and exposed means you have to stay fit—that is, stay

true—because when you're walking around, other people are looking at you.

Being open fosters responsibility in an organization. People can see what you're doing and scrutinize everything you do. For example, if an open company were destroying the environment and people could see that, their C-level executives would make different decisions because they're being scrutinized, versus if everything were hidden and nobody knew what was going on until it was too late.

The safety issue that BP Oil was going through is one example. If the company were open and people could see that they weren't following safety processes, it would have prevented this big disaster for the company—a disaster that cost them billions of dollars. I'm sure nobody in BP Oil set out to intentionally strive to skip or overlook safety issues and let it fall apart on purpose. But regardless, it created an environment where responsibility to the environment wasn't seen as a big deal for senior management or its workers.

Responsibility is an effect of being open. It's a cause and effect. If a company is an open one, it will naturally will become a more responsible one, as well—if not voluntarily, then because others are holding the company's proverbial feet to the fire. It forces a company's employees and its C-suite to become more accountable.

The process of responsibility does not rely on one person, but a group of people.

In an open environment, everyone is responsible, but the CEO sets the tone for creating a culture that drives responsibility.

How does this relate to corporate profits? Corporate profit is a big piece, but it's not the total picture. There are different pieces. If a company is doing something responsible, but it's not contributing to corporate profit, that's not going to do anybody any good because the corporation's goal is basically making money. That's why the company was started. So the responsibility process of it is to make profits without sacrificing other things, like employee welfare and customer welfare.

For example, if you have the greatest product on earth, but you have lead paint on it, it's not going to do your customers any good. Actually, it could harm them. You could make the best profits in the world but you lost the sense of responsibility to your customers to deliver a safe product. Safety is a byproduct of responsibility—including safety for the consumer, the employees, the community, and the environment.

Going back to the previous example with Walmart offering a $12 T-shirt: If their customers understood that a different process could be used that would save 5,000 gallons of water, a segment of their customer base that is concerned with the environment might likely be willing to pay more for that T-shirt, because it contributes to the larger goal of sustainability.

Consumers know that a company is for profit. They have no problem paying for a particular product, or the fact that the company will make money on it. But *how* a company makes its profit and all that's entailed is important.

Profit is absolutely necessary. However, a company with a culture of responsibility knows that they can make a fair profit, while also being responsible to the environment and doing that in such a way that customers feel good about buying the product.

The Walmart T-shirt example is hypothetical. Can a company really make a profit if being responsible drives up the price of their goods or services? Absolutely. One only needs to look to Starbucks® for proof. Starbucks advertises their fair-trade process. Can they get their coffee cheaper? Sure, they can. They can squeeze the farmers in developing countries to get a cheaper price. However, they've opted for a fair-trade process that pays farmers to be more responsible to the environment. This allows the farmers to make a profit they can live on, while caring for the environment and providing superior products to their consumers.

The fact that people will pay $4 for a cup of coffee is proof that it can work. In the 70s, if you told somebody that a cup of coffee would cost them $4, they would pass out—nobody would pay more than 50 cents for a cup of coffee at that time. Fair trade marketing openly shows consumers what creating their cup of coffee entails and how Starbucks can both deliver a superior product and be responsible company to their grower supply chain.

Responsibility is a competitive advantage. Look at all of the bad publicity that Walmart got around not paying fair wages and having employees who are on food stamps. The corporate profits were good, but at the same time, they weren't being a responsible company to their employees. The bad publicity they got cost them a lot of money and a lot of profits because many thought they weren't paying a fair living wage. They recently announced that they're raising wages for all of their employees. They didn't do that because they wanted to—it was due to all of the pressure they have been getting. To add insult to injury, they were being compared to Costco® and other retailers who are paying their employees a lot more and providing health insurance. This comparison gave Costco free advertisement and great PR—highlighting their corporate responsibility—while Walmart fared poorly in the public sphere.

In the age of blogs and citizen journalism, scrutiny of corporate practices can transcend mainstream media. One negative review can go viral and be seen my millions in a very short time. The negative opinions can then escalate from one person to hundreds of thousands ... truly, this form of negative advertisement can have a far greater impact on public opinion than a high-profile multi-million dollar marketing campaign. But when a company chooses responsibility, they are less likely to be subjected to negative feedback, which can then help the company grow their process, instead of scrambling to do damage control.

Corporate responsibility always affects a company's brand and manifests itself through that company's treatment of its employees, its products, and the actions the company takes. How do people learn whether a company exercises this sense of responsibility? The company doesn't necessarily have to advertise or promote it. If the company is open and transparent, people will find out.

Effective responsibility can find itself in a two-way dialogue with public opinion. An example, although controversial, is a mom-and-pop cake shop that announced they wouldn't create wedding cakes for the LGBT community. As word got out, people started to boycott their business. It took them only a few months to go out of business. The trends and mainstream public opinion in the U.S. on LGBT rights and gay marriage had shifted. The bakery owners took a stand, they said, based on their religious values, and the larger public—and enough of the bakery's customer base—took a counteractive stand based on discrimination and civil rights, the latter succeeding in shutting the business down. In this case, it is apparent that a corporation is not a leader of public opinion—on the contrary, public opinion can sometimes call the values of a corporation into question, and ultimately prevail by affecting a company's bottom line—and very existence.

Now that stakeholders—including consumers, investors, and employees—pay increasing attention to the social and environmental footprints of business, corporate-responsibility efforts have moved into uncharted management territory. We see companies reengineering supply chains to make them "greener," supporting social causes through volunteer programs for employees, or lobbying for human rights in far-flung corners of the globe.

As this tide swells, many executives are left with the nagging sense that such investments rest on a shaky understanding of how corporate responsibility creates value, both for their companies and for society. Some investments, of course, produce immediate and quantifiable gains, such as those from recycling or from manufacturing processes that save energy. But often, social investments are expected to yield longer-term benefits as engaged consumers step up their purchases, a broader investor base develops, or new talent flocks to a company's recruiters.

In more ambiguous cases, how is a manager to know whether stakeholders will indeed respond positively? Research, described in greater detail in our recent book, *Leveraging Corporate Responsibility: The Stakeholder Route to Maximizing Business and Social Value,* suggests that while stakeholders' interpretations of corporate responsibility are multifaceted, it is vital that managers avoid creating an impression that such activities are crowding out core business priorities. In fact, some well-meaning corporate-responsibility activities can actually harm a company's competitiveness.

Consider an experiment: Consumers were asked to rate their own purchase intentions for computer accessories with several companies after learning about their product quality and corporate-responsibility activities. A modest positive effect resulted when a company was described as having high quality products. A company with low product quality didn't benefit at all by informing consumers of their otherwise positive corporate responsibility activities. In fact, consumer willingness to buy from them actually decreased. Why? Consumers were wary of these activities, thinking that the company ought to give precedence to product quality. Related research shows a similar dynamic at work with investors: highly innovative Fortune 1000 companies derive greater financial returns from their corporate-responsibility activities than their less innovative counterparts do.

By following a few basic principles, leaders can increase the likelihood that stakeholders will interpret corporate-responsibility initiatives as they intend for them to be conveyed—and, hopefully, more positively.

Don't hide market motives: Stakeholders are remarkably open to the business case for corporate responsibility, as long as initiatives are appropriate, given what stakeholders know about a company's strategic vision, and as long as that company genuinely pursues and achieves an endeavor accompanying social value. Companies should understand that they can pursue profitable core business and corporate-responsibility objectives in tandem, without trade-offs.

Serve stakeholders' true needs: Consumers are drawn to products that satisfy their needs. Likewise, stakeholders are drawn to companies whose corporate-responsibility activities produce solid benefits, which can be tangible (such as improved health in local communities) or less tangible (for instance, volunteer programs that help employees better integrate their work and home lives). Before investing in corporate responsibility, senior managers and other decision makers need to set clear objectives that their company can meet, and then, ideally, create programs together with key stakeholder groups.

Test your progress: Corporate responsibility acts as a conduit through which companies can demonstrate that they care about their stakeholders. A company should assess its initiatives regularly to ensure that they foster the desired unity between its own goals and those of stakeholders. Calibrating strategy frequently improves the odds that corporate responsibility will create value for all parties.

The Value of Responsibility

Evidence links socially responsible business practices to improved financial performance. This is attributable to lower costs or increased revenue from customers who want to support a business that reflects their personal values. An organization's corporate social responsibility practices might also increase employee loyalty, which lowers the cost of turnover. It also helps attract potential employees willing to work for less for a company whose values they share.

Some corporate social responsibility actions, such as investing in renewable energy, can provide tax benefits or lead to technological innovations that create competitive advantages.

Harvard professors Michael Porter and Mark Kramer introduced the notion of "creating shared value" (CSV) as a way of thinking about the benefits of corporate social responsibility. CSV is based on the idea that the competitiveness of a company and the health of the communities around it are mutually dependent. By focusing on creating shared value, an organization helps to shape the context in which it competes to its advantage. In this way, the shared value model takes a long-term perspective on the financial benefits of corporate social responsibility.

Other financial benefits from corporate social responsibility accrue directly to shareholders. Socially conscious investors may prefer to own shares of a company that demonstrates good corporate social responsibility, which can lead to higher share prices. Some mutual funds have portfolios exclusively made up of companies that rate highly on independent corporate social responsibility measures. Proponents of these funds point to competitive returns for socially responsible indices, such as the Domini 400 (now the MSCI KLD 400). Similarly, academic studies have shown that excluding stocks from companies with poor corporate social responsibility records does not adversely affect financial returns of a fund.

Socially responsible corporate performance can be associated with a series of bottom-line benefits. However, in many cases, the time span between costs and benefits may seem out of alignment—the costs are immediate, and the benefits don't often appear in time for quarterly earnings results. Nevertheless, many other benefits can be identified.

First, socially responsible companies have an enhanced brand image and reputation. Consumers are often drawn to brands and companies with good reputations in corporate social responsibility-related issues. A company regarded as socially responsible can also benefit from its reputation within the business community by having an increased ability to attract capital and trading partners. A reputation is hard to quantify and measure, and even harder to measure how much it increases a company's value. However, since companies have developed methods to measure the benefits of their advertisement campaigns, similar methods can, and should, be applied to corporate reputations.

There are also other cases in which doing what is good and responsible converges with doing what's best for a particular business. Some corporate social responsibility initiatives can dramatically reduce operating costs. For example, reducing packaging material or planning the optimum route for delivery trucks not only reduces the environmental impact of a company's operation, but it also reduces some of its variable costs.

The process of adopting corporate social responsibility principles motivates executives to reconsider their business practices, and to seek more efficient ways of operating. Companies perceived to have a strong corporate social responsibility commitment often have an increased ability to attract and retain employees[1], which leads to reduced turnover, recruitment, and training costs. Employees, too,

---

[1] Turban & Greening, 1997

often evaluate their companies' corporate social responsibility performance to determine if their personal values conflict with those of the businesses at which they work. There are many known cases in which employees were asked, under pressure of their supervisors, to overlook written or moral laws in order to achieve higher profits. These practices created a culture of fear in the workplace and harmed employees' trust, loyalty, and commitment to their employers.

Companies that improve working conditions and labor practices also experience increased productivity and reduced error rates. Regular controls in a company's global production helps to ensure that all its employees work under good conditions and earn living wages. These practices can be costly, but the increased productivity of workers and improved quality of products can generate positive cash flows that can cover associated costs. Thus, firms may actually benefit from socially responsible actions in terms of employee morale and productivity[2].

Based on analysis of archival internal tobacco-industry documents, generated from 2000 to 2002, related to discussions of corporate social responsibility among a Corporate Responsibility Taskforce and senior management at Philip Morris® in exploring corporate social responsibility, Philip Morris executives sought to identify the company's social value—its positive contribution to society. Struggling to find an answer, they considered dramatically changing the way the company marketed its products, apologizing for past actions, and committing the company to providing benefits for future generations. These ideas were eventually abandoned. Despite an initial

---

[2] Moskowitz, 1972; Parket & Eibert, 1975; Soloman & Hansen, 1985

call to distinguish between social and economic value, Philip Morris ultimately equated social value with providing shareholder returns.

When even tobacco executives struggle to define their company's social value, it signals an opening to advocate for end-game scenarios that would encourage supply-side changes appropriate to the scale of the tobacco disease epidemic and consistent with authentic social value.

4

CULTURE OF
INFORMATION

*"Information about the package is as important
as the package itself."*

Frederick W. Smith

ALONG WITH A CULTURE OF RESPONSIBILITY, AN OPEN
organization also fosters a culture of transparency. This
applies to the flow of transparent information within a
company, as well as sharing information between
companies.

In the past, companies have taken a secretive stance, rather
than an open and unshrouded one. This was based on a
philosophy of: *The less people know, the more power
corporate decision-makers retain.* This trend has been
changing over time, largely due to the access to information
that some employees and customers have. Let's not forget
that your employees and whistleblowers are part of your
company, and if there is no transparency in the company, it
will impede progress.

Before we delve too far into the culture of transparent information, it's important to understand that there are different types of information. One is the information that is patentable and helps the innovation process. Other types of information include personnel information, such as salaries and benefits, profits, costs of materials, supplies, and labor, internal goals and values, suppliers, investments, and corporate responsibility efforts and their results.

Culture of Transparency

You need to insert introductory text leading up to these concepts. It's also hard for me to edit this section without the lead-up text letting the reader know what each of these sections is illustrating.

Fake transparency: Shared salary information is one manifestation of transparency. However, what I've noticed is a trend of half-way salary transparency masquerading as full transparency. It's better than complete secrecy, for sure, but it's just not enough, and this pertains to founders and managing directors who are perhaps failing their own ideals by thinking this is actual transparency, when it's not. It also affects recruitment and the perception that both prospective hires and existing employees have when they notice the cognitive dissonance between stated transparency and lack thereof.

Trust but verify: When our belief systems migrated from religious and mythical, mostly handled by priests, to scientific and secular, one of the most tangible-differences was a shift from a system of trust—where information from an authority figure was often accepted, unquestioned—to a system of verified facts, where everyone could, and was invited to, examine statements and test theories for themselves.

One of the primary ways that transparency creates trust is that everyone knows that they have accurate information. They don't have to take it on blind trust; they can check it themselves. Now, unlike high-speed relativistic physics, there is nothing in your typical business records that cannot be understood by the layman, with some fairly basic training and explanations.

The ability to verify the knowledge you rely on, rather than accept it as handed down by an authority figure, is so powerful, so transformational, that it turned the world upside down and is largely responsible for the way the world works today. A society where the people cannot verify information for themselves, where the government hides things from them, is one headed for totalitarianism.

The same is true within business. Being able to verify that what you know is actually true, rather than rely on faith alone, is a fundamental feature and benefit of transparency, a huge driver of the increased trust that is typical of open cultures.

Unverifiable Data is NOT Transparent

Many companies claim to have transparent salaries, but when you scratch the surface, you find out that what they have are transparent salary bands. Now, that's a starting point, but it is not at all the same as having transparent salaries. Any company that says "we have transparent salaries" but has only a transparent salary scheme is likely to be hiding something, for the simple reason that compensation is a really sensitive, high-pressure topic where employees may automatically apply tricks and tactics.

Any "transparent salary bands" system will almost immediately be corrupted by people who will apply the right pressure to the right points and argue convincingly that they don't quite fit within the regular bands and deserve some sort of premium. Soon enough, you end up with a majority of people on the transparent scheme, and a small but growing number of people with special deals. Those deals are allowed to exist because they are hidden.

If a company has a "transparent" compensation scheme, but doesn't actively publish its accounting and payroll data internally, you can bet your bottom dollar that there are people with special deals in the system. Know for a fact there is unfairness in the system. Apart from all sorts of other impacts, it means that you will be wanting to get your own special deal, as well. I'd wager that your average "transparent salary bands" system has a sizeable minority (20 – 30% at least) of its staff on special deals. In other words, it does not have salary transparency at all.

This is the only viable way to do salary transparency: Fully open up the financial data.

If you want to get the full benefits of transparency, you must make the critically important compensation system transparent. If you don't, then unfairness will creep into the system via this critical channel and build up over time. You can keep fighting it, but it will sap your energy, and eventually you'll give in.

The best time to implement salary and financial information transparency is on day one if you're a startup— when there is no unfairness in the system yet. If you wait until a lot of this unfairness has built up, shining a light on it may well be politically unfeasible. You may find you have to choose between transparency and losing some of your best people (who are the most likely to have successfully argued for special deals), while demolishing company morale for a while.

The same flaws that affect verifiability in science can affect verifiability in financial information. Namely, things can become too complex for anyone but a small cabal of (compensation) experts to understand. Or maybe the company has twenty thousand people and a supposedly transparent, but hard-to-access payroll information system.

If the information is not easily accessible, it is also not transparent. And as information becomes more complex, it inevitably becomes harder to access. So, even if you do have completely transparent and easily accessible financial data, it will take some consistent effort to keep things that way as the company grows. Bear that in mind and don't let inaccessibility creep in through complexity or other access issues.

If you want to unveil salary information in your own company, where do you start?

First, See Where You Stand

Before key decision makers in your firm dive into completely sharing compensation data, they have to fully embrace the concept.

Going halfway can be dangerous. "If you go part way with it, it still leaves the door open to mistrust, and to a toxic environment. If employees have tasted transparency on other levels within your firm, they're going to be very aware of the lack of transparency in salaries.

When questions don't get answers, naturally, people make up their own answers. They fill in the gaps for what's not transparent. And that's where the danger lies.

Leader Check Thyself: Are You Personally Transparent?

To determine your personal transparency level, start with a simple—yet potentially challenging—test, particularly for founders and C-level leaders. It's very simple, but it does require your full honesty. Just ask yourself a critical question: Do you share with friends openly? If someone asks you what your salary is right now, are you reluctant to share that?"

If you hesitate, it requires further soul searching and reflection before you continue to the next step. If you're confident you would, that doesn't mean you're ready to disclose salaries, but you're off to a great start.

What's most important is your mindset—that you know and are aware that sharing things with others, keeping few or no secrets, is the right thing to do.

Maybe just as crucial is putting your worries to bed. What is the worst that could happen? And in all reality, is it just possible that the "worst" is highly unlikely to come into play—and the alternative, which is being transparent, has benefits that are stronger than your worries and fears.

The biggest fear is that someone will steal our secrets. Competition is a word I hear a lot. Not everyone is copying you. Everything keeps on going. Dealing with your fear isn't merely trying to convince yourself that your fear has no merit; it's more of an emotional learning. Take time to really explore your emotions first.

The Benefits of Transparency

While this book has discussed how transparency, or the lack of it, can help or hurt a company, it's important to know the specific benefits that a company can expect to gain when they implement a culture of transparency. Among the main benefits and those which are most likely to affect the majority of companies are:

Efficiency: The awareness among the entire team of what is happening within the company on all levels allows everyone to pitch in where it makes the most sense. A clearly defined set of values paired with transparency means you'll be looking for very specific candidates, easing the often-painful hiring process.

Loyalty: Whether it is employees, customers, or potential hires, honesty and information creates a relationship that makes them more vested. Buffer's® largest sign-up days and biggest application batches have come when it's released transparency posts on fundraising, revenue, and salaries.

Greater trust: As mentioned before, your employees are going to fill in the gaps of information it doesn't know. If they're treated responsibly and given accurate information, it's easier for them to get behind the company's mission.

Reduced stress: When employees know where they, their co-workers, and the company stand at all times, there's far less uncertainty. Uncertainty leads to stress, which lends itself to lost time and employees who are unhappy, not satisfied, and less productive.

This process also equals the playing field for women and minorities. They do not have to worry about being paid less than their peers since the information is open.

Open Systems Win!

Open systems win. This is counter-intuitive to the traditionally trained MBA who is taught to generate a sustainable competitive advantage by creating a closed system, making it popular, then milking it through the product life cycle. The conventional wisdom goes that companies should lock in customers to lock out competitors.

There are different tactical approaches — razor companies make the razor cheap and the blades expensive, while the old IBM made the mainframes expensive and the software, well, it was expensive, too. Either way, a well-managed closed system can deliver plenty of profit.

It can also deliver well-designed products in the short run— the iPod and iPhone being the obvious examples—but eventually, innovation in a closed system tends toward being incremental at best (is a four-blade razor really that much better than one with three blades?) because the whole point is to preserve what already works—proven quantities. Complacency is the hallmark of any closed system. If you don't have to work that hard to keep your customers, you won't.

Open systems are just the opposite. They are competitive and far more dynamic. In an open system, a competitive advantage doesn't derive from locking in customers, but rather from understanding the fast-moving system better than anyone else and using that knowledge to generate better, more innovative products. The successful company in an open system is both a fast innovator and a thought leader. The brand value of thought leadership attracts customers and then fast innovation keeps them. This isn't easy—far from it—but fast companies have nothing to fear, and when they are successful, they can generate great shareholder value.

Open systems have the potential to spawn industries. They harness the intellect of the general population and spur businesses to compete, innovate, and win based on the merits of their products, not just the brilliance of their business tactics. The race to map the human genome is one example.

In the book *Wikinomics*, Don Tapscott and Anthony Williams explain how in the mid-1990s private firms were discovering and patenting large amounts of DNA sequence data and then assuming control over who could access that information and at what price.

Having so much of the genome under private ownership raised costs and made drug discovery far less efficient. Then, in 1995, Merck Pharmaceuticals® and the Gene Sequencing Center at Washington University changed the game by creating a new, open initiative called the Merck Gene Index. It gave researchers everywhere unrestricted access to an open resource of genetic information.

Within three years, they had published over 800,000 gene sequences into the public domain, and soon other collaborative projects followed suit. This was in an industry where early-stage R&D was traditionally pursued individually in closed labs, so Merck's open approach not only changed the culture of the entire field, it also accelerated the pace of biomedical research and drug development.

Another way to look at the difference between open and closed systems is that open systems allow innovation at all levels—from the operating system to the application layer—not just at the top. This means that one company doesn't have to depend on another's benevolence to ship a product. If the GNU C compiler that I'm using has a bug, I can fix it since the compiler is open source. I don't have to file a bug report and hope for a timely response.

So if you are trying to grow an entire industry as broadly as possible, open systems trump closed. And that is exactly what is happening with the Internet. Our commitment to open systems is not altruistic. Rather, it's good business, since an open Internet creates a steady stream of innovations that attracts users and usage, and grows the entire industry. Hal Varian has an equation in his book, *Information Rules*, that applies here:

$$\text{Reward} = (\text{Total value added to the industry})$$
$$\times (\text{Our share of industry value})$$

All other things being equal, a 10-percent increase in share or a 10- percent increase in industry value should lead to the same outcome. But in IT, a 10 percent increase in industry value will yield a much bigger reward, because it will stimulate economies of scale across the entire industry, increasing productivity and reducing costs for all competitors. As long as we contribute a steady stream of great products, we will prosper along with the entire ecosystem. We may get a smaller piece, but it will come from a bigger pie.

In other words, the future depends on the Internet staying an open system, and our advocacy of open will grow the web for everyone.

Open Information

The foundation of open standards and open source has led to a Web where massive amounts of personal information—photos, contacts, updates—are regularly uploaded. The scale of information being shared, and the fact that it can be saved forever, creates a question that was hardly a consideration a few years ago: How do we treat this information?

Historically, new information technologies have often enabled new forms of commerce. For example, when traders in the Mediterranean region circa 3000 BC invented seals (called bullae) to ensure that their shipments reached their destinations tamper-free, they transformed commerce from local to long distance. Similar transformations were spurred by the advent of the written word, and more recently, computers. At every step of the way the transaction, a consensual agreement where each party gets something of value, was powered by a new type of information that allowed a contract to be enforced.

On the Web, the new form of commerce is the exchange of personal information for something of value. This is a transaction that millions of us participate in every day, and it has potentially great benefits. An auto insurer could monitor a customer's driving habits in real-time and give a discount for good driving—or charge a premium for speeding —powered by information (GPS tracking) that wasn't available only a few years ago. This is a fairly simple transaction, but we will encounter far more sensitive scenarios.

Let's say your child has an allergy to certain medicines. Would you allow her medical data to be accessible by a smart wireless syringe which could prevent an emergency medical technician or nurse from accidentally giving her that medicine? I would, but you might decide the metal bracelet around her wrist is sufficient. And that's the point: people can, and will, reach different decisions on myriad things, and when it comes to personal information, we need to treat all of those decisions with equal respect.

While having more personal information online can be quite beneficial to everyone, its uses should be guided by principles that are responsible, scalable, and flexible enough to grow and change over time. And unlike open technology, where our objective is to grow the Internet ecosystem, our approach to open information is to build trust with the individuals who engage within that ecosystem (users, partners, and customers). Trust is the most important currency online, so to build it, one should adhere to three principles of open information: value, transparency, and control:

Value: First and foremost is the need to make products that are valuable to users. In many cases, we can make our products even better if we know more information about the user, but privacy concerns can arise if people don't understand what value they are getting in return for their information. Explain that value to them, however, and they will often agree to the transaction. For example, millions of people let credit card companies retain information on the purchases they make with their card in exchange for the convenience of not carrying around cash.

This should be the default approach: tell people, in obvious, plain language, what we need to know about them, and why it's valuable to them that we know it. Do you think that your product's value is so obvious that it doesn't need explaining? There's a good chance you're wrong. Explain the value so you know with all certainty that they are aware of your product's value.

Transparency: Next, is the need to make it easy for users to find out what information you gather and store about them across all of your products.

If you manage a consumer product where you collect information from your users, your product should be part of the dashboard, telling users what you are collecting and for what purpose. If you're already there, you're not done. With every new feature or version, ask yourself if you have any additional information (maybe even information that is publicly available about users on other sites) that you can add to your dashboard. The fact of the matter is, if you don't make the information you collect public knowledge, people will be skeptical and, yes, fearful of your company and its motives.

Think about how you can increase transparency within your product, as well. When you download an Android app, for example, the device tells you what information the app will be able to access about you and your phone, and then you get to decide whether or not to proceed. You don't have to dig deep to figure out what information you are divulging. Is your product that transparent? Do you immediately disclose up front what information you can access and why? How can you use transparency to your advantage and increase users' engagement with your product by increasing transparency?

Control: Finally, you must always give control to the user. If you have information about a user, as with IBA, it should be easy for the user to delete that information and opt-out. If users access your products and store content with you, it's their content, not yours. They should be able to export it or delete it at any time, at no cost, and as easily as possible. Gmail is a great example of this, since Google offers free forwarding to any address. The ability to switch is critical, so instead of building walls around your product, build bridges. Give users real options.

If there are existing standards for handling user data, you should adhere to them. If a standard doesn't exist, you should work to create an open one that benefits the entire web, even if a closed standard appears to be better for you (remember—it's not!). In the meantime, you need to do whatever you can to make leaving your company as easy as possible for users. Your company should not be like Hotel California—you can check out any time you like and you CAN, in fact, leave!

As Eric Schmitt of Google said in his 2009 strategy memo, "We don't trap users, we make it easy for them to move to our competitors." This policy is similar to the emergency exits on an airplane—an analogy that your pilot CEO would appreciate. You hope to never use them, but you're glad they're there, and would be furious if they weren't. That analogy helps us to better understand that your customers would also be furious if they were locked in and had no way out.

Build your products so that the exporting of data is easy. One way you can do this is by having a good public API (application program interface) that exposes all of your users' data. Don't wait for version 2.0 or 3.0. Discuss this early in your product planning meetings, and make it a feature of your product from the start.

When reporters at the *Guardian*, a leading U.K. newspaper, reviewed the work of the Data Liberation team from Google, they proclaimed it to be "counter-intuitive" for those "accustomed to the lock-in mentality of previous commercial battles." They are right; it is counterintuitive to people who are stuck in the old MBA way of thinking, but if you do your homework, soon it won't be. The goal is to open the default. People will gravitate toward it, then they will expect and demand it, and be unhappy when they don't get it. When open is intuitive, we all have succeeded.

Open will win. It will win on the Internet and will then cascade across many walks of life. The future of government is transparency. The future of commerce is information symmetry. The future of culture is freedom. The future of science and medicine is collaboration. The future of entertainment is participation. Each of these futures depends on an open Internet.

The extent of your company's open culture is entirely up to its leaders—the CEO and C-Suite-level executives who are the decision makers and who frame the company's vision, mission, goals, and the reputation you desire among your employees, suppliers, customers, community, and around the world.

Until recently, the yardstick used to evaluate the performance of American corporate leaders was relatively simple: the extent to which they created wealth for investors. But that was then. Now the forces of globalization and technology have conspired to complicate the competitive arena, creating a need for leaders who can manage rapid innovation. Expectations about the corporation's role in social issues, such as environmental degradation, domestic job creation, and even poverty in the developing world, have risen sharply, as well. And the expedient, short-term thinking that Wall Street rewarded what seems like only yesterday has fallen out of fashion in the wake of the latest round of business busts and scandals.

It's clear we need a better way to evaluate business leaders. Moving forward, it appears that the new metric of corporate leadership will be closer to this: the extent to which executives create organizations that are economically, ethically, and socially sustainable.

How can leaders accomplish such an ambitious task? Their action plans will vary, of course, depending on the nature of their industries, the peculiarities of their companies, and the unique challenges they face. But whatever their strategies and tactics, we believe prudent leaders will see that increased transparency is a fundamental first step.

When we speak of transparency, we are referring to much more than the standard business definition of the term—full disclosure of financial information to investors. While such honesty is obviously necessary, that narrow interpretation produces an unhealthy focus on legal compliance to the exclusion of equally important ethical concerns, and on the needs of shareholders to the exclusion of the needs of other constituencies. Worse, it's predicated on the blinkered assumption that a company can be transparent to shareholders without first being transparent to the people who work inside it. Because no organization can be honest with the public if it's not honest with itself, we define transparency broadly, as the degree to which information flows freely within an organization, among managers and employees, and outward to stakeholders.

How Openness Improves Performance

Admittedly, the relationship between organizational openness and performance is complex, but it's worth examining from a number of angles: whether people who need to communicate upward are able to do so easily and honestly; whether teams are able to challenge their own assumptions openly; and whether boards of directors are able to communicate important messages to the company's leadership.

We'll tackle upward communication first. Consider the results of an intriguing, relatively obscure study from the

1980s, in which organizational theorists Robert Blake and Jane Mouton examined NASA's findings on the human factors involved in airline accidents. NASA researchers had placed existing cockpit crews—pilot, co-pilot, navigator—in flight simulators and tested them to see how they would respond during the crucial 30 to 45 seconds between the first sign of a potential accident and the moment it would occur. The stereotypical take-charge "flyboy" pilots, who acted immediately on their gut instincts, made the wrong decisions far more often than the more open, inclusive pilots who said to their crews, in effect, "We've got a problem. How do you read it?" before choosing a course of action.

At one level, the lesson of the NASA findings is simple: Leaders are far likelier to make mistakes when they act on too little information than when they wait to learn more. But Blake and Mouton went deeper, demonstrating that the pilots' habitual style of interacting with their crews determined whether crew members would provide them with essential information during an in-air crisis. The pilots who'd made the right choices routinely had open exchanges with their crew members. The study also showed that crew members who had regularly worked with the "decisive" pilots were unwilling to intervene—even when they had information that might save the plane.

That kind of silence has a tremendous price. In his recent book, *Outliers*, Malcolm Gladwell reviewed data from numerous airline accidents. "The kinds of errors that cause plane crashes are invariably errors of teamwork and communication," he concluded. "One pilot knows something important and somehow doesn't tell the other pilot." Hence, in an emergency pilots need to "communicate not just in the sense of issuing commands but also in the sense of...sharing information in the clearest and most transparent manner possible."

Transparency problems don't always involve a leader who won't listen to followers (or followers who won't speak up). They also arise when members of a team suffer from groupthink—they don't know how to disagree with one another. This second type of problem has been written about a lot, but it's very much alive in the executive meeting rooms of large corporations. Shared values and assumptions play a positive and necessary role in holding any group together. But when a team of senior managers suffer from collective denial and self-deception—when they can't unearth and question their shared assumptions—they can't innovate or make course corrections effectively. That often leads to business and ethical disasters.

While groupthink may, in part, be the result of like minds who tend to agree or find it easier to agree than to counter an opinion or suggestion, it may also be possible that groupthink is the byproduct of the "team" framework that encourages employees to be a team player and work well with others. Working well together is always important, especially with key decision makers; but being a team member should never override the curiosity and desire to make the right decisions based on the information at hand. When it does, there is a tendency for curiosity, and therefore, change and innovation to be stifled. As a result, too often, the status quo is maintained. The vital information that can stem from true transparency disclosed in an environment where individuals are willing to challenge processes and policies is lost.

We've argued for more transparency for a long time—but the truth is, we haven't seen much progress. In the combined fourscore and 10 years we've been studying organizations, the most common metaphor we've heard managers use to describe their own cultures is "a mushroom farm"—as in, *People around here are kept in the dark and fed manure.* When we recently polled 154 executives, 63% of them described their own company culture as opaque. And the remaining 37% were more likely to choose clouds over bright sunshine to describe the communication practices at their firms.

Organizational transparency makes sense rationally and ethically, and it makes businesses run more efficiently and effectively. But, even so, leaders resist it, because it goes against the grain of group behavior, and, in some ways, even against human nature. In all groups, leaders try to hoard and control information because they believe it's a source of power. Managers sometimes believe that access to information is a perquisite of power, a benefit that separates their privileged caste from the hoi polloi. Such leaders apparently feel that they're smarter than their followers, and thus only they need, or would know how to use, sensitive and complex information. Some even like opacity because it allows them to hide embarrassing mistakes.

A third type of transparency problem occurs when the board of directors abdicates its responsibility to provide genuine oversight. An alarming number of board members today seem to succumb to the "shimmer effect"—they let charismatic CEOs get away with blatantly poor decisions and action (or outrageous greed, at any rate). Witness the behavior of Hollinger International's former CEO Conrad Black, who spent some $8 million of his shareholders' funds to treat himself to a private collection of Franklin D. Roosevelt memorabilia. Worse, Black was found guilty of taking millions in illegal payments for agreeing not to compete with Hollinger's own subsidiaries. Overall, it was estimated that more than $800 million in assets was improperly spent or used by Black. However, the company's board, which included Henry Kissinger, held Black in such awe that it simply did not provide prudent oversight. What Black and his board failed to factor into their pact of silence is that truth has a way of ultimately surfacing.

Why Transparency is Inevitable Today

What executives are learning, often the hard way, is that their ability to keep secrets is vanishing—in large part because of the Internet. This is true not just in open democracies but in authoritarian states, as well. For example, in 2007, blogger Lian Yue warned residents of Xiamen, China, of plans to build a chemical plant in their beautiful coastal city. Even a decade earlier, the factory would have been built before local citizens were the wiser. But urged on by Lian, opposition spread quickly in Xiamen, via e-mail, blogs, and text messages. Protesters organized a march on the town's city hall to demand the cancellation of the project. Although government censors promptly shut down their websites, the protesters took photos of the demonstration with their cell phones and sent them to journalists. A million messages opposing the plant reportedly were circulated. The government ultimately agreed to do an environmental impact study, and the plant was moved 30 miles out of town.

If this can happen in China, it can happen anywhere. Today anyone with a cell phone and access to a computer could conceivably stand up to a billion-dollar corporation. Trying to restrict the free flow of information doesn't work for corporate executives any more than it did for government officials in Xiamen. An instructive example is the decision of medical manufacturer, Guidant®, not to publicize a defect it discovered in some models of its defibrillators. The flaw caused a small number of the implanted heart regulators to short-circuit and malfunction. However, according to reports in *The New York Times,* Guidant executives didn't tell doctors about it for three years. They remained silent until the spring of 2005, when one of the devices was implicated in the death of a college student, whose physicians contacted the *Times.*

Though it was under fire, Guidant didn't recall the defibrillators for almost another month—and not until another death had been connected to its product. Eventually, the Guidant devices were implicated in at least five more deaths, and the result was a catastrophic trust problem with the company's primary customers: physicians. Guidant's share of the defibrillator market dropped from 35% to about 24% after the recall, apparently because of the disgust many doctors felt over the company's decision to conceal the truth.

In stark contrast to Guidant, some farsighted leaders institute a "no secrets" policy designed to build trust among all corporate stakeholders. Kent Thiry, CEO of DaVita®, a dialysis-treatment operator, systematically collects data and solicits candid feedback from his employees, ex-employees, customers, and suppliers, in order to guide his decision making. Thiry actively seeks out bad news and rewards employees who give it to him.

To reinforce trust, he and his top managers act promptly to correct practices that employees have identified as problematic—issues that, if left unchecked, could come back to haunt the company. And unusual historical examples of similar displays of openness that created public trust companies as diverse as Honeywell®, Continental Airlines®, Johnson & Johnson®, Nordstrom®, Whole Foods®, and Xilinx® are the stuff of legend.

Creating Transparency

A culture of openness doesn't just develop on its own—the hoarding of information is far too persistent in organizations of all kinds. That said, leaders can take steps to create and nurture transparency. The bottom line with each of these recommendations is that leaders need to be role models—they must share more information, look for counterarguments, admit their own errors, and behave as they want others to behave:

Tell the Truth: When followers are asked to rank what they need from their leaders, trustworthiness almost always tops the list. Leaders who are candid and predictable—they tell everyone the same thing and don't continually revise their stories—signal to followers that the rules of the game aren't changing and that decisions won't be made arbitrarily. Given that assurance, followers become more willing to stick their necks out, make an extra effort, and put themselves on the line to help their leaders achieve goals.

Encourage people to speak truth to power: Building trust takes time and consistency, and the reward is an unimpeded flow of intelligence. Sometimes that includes news and information that executives don't want to hear. Clearheaded managers appreciate such openness. As one shared, "The only messenger I would ever shoot is one who arrived too late." Many executives are not that enlightened, however. What they fail to understand is that trust is a symbiotic relationship: Leaders first must trust others before others will trust them.

It's never easy for employees to be honest with their bosses. After a string of box office flops, movie mogul Samuel Goldwyn had a meeting with his top staff and reportedly said, "I don't want any yes-men around me. I want everybody to tell me the truth even if it costs them their jobs." The story illustrates that speaking truth to power requires both a willing listener and a courageous speaker.

In all organizations—families, sports teams, schools, businesses, and government agencies—those lower down in the pecking order may experience, from time to time, the terror involved in having to tell unpalatable truths to those above them. Daring to speak truth to power often entails considerable risk—whether at the hands of an irate parent, a neighborhood bully, or an incensed movie studio boss. There is the fear that the messenger can lose favor, even though the leader encouraged them to speak up.

Naturally, there is also a concern that the employee who is forthright in disclosing information may be held liable for it or the recipient of the dissatisfaction felt by higher ups. We commonly refer to this fear when we say, "Don't shoot the messenger." What would one do if, although the leaders encourage employees to divulge what they know and speak freely, they were met with anger and angst?

Imagine the courage it would have taken for an Enron® employee to confront Jeffrey Skilling with the facts of the company's financial deception. Or, even the courage required by a GE employee simply to question the company's former CEO, Jack Welch. According to *Fortune*, former GE employees reported that "Welch conducts meetings so aggressively that people tremble. He attacks almost physically with his intellect—criticizing, demeaning, ridiculing, humiliating."

In the early 1970s, Albert O. Hirschman posited that employees who disagree with company policy have only three options: exit, voice, or loyalty. That is, they can offer a principled resignation (exit), try to change the policy (voice truth to power), or remain team players despite their opposition (loyalty). Even today, most people choose option three—the path of least resistance. They swallow whatever objections they may have to questionable dictates from above, concluding that they lack the power to change things or, worse, will be punished if they try. Most executives expect their people to be good soldiers and not question company policy, but a great leader will welcome alternative viewpoints.

Reward contrarians: Companies with healthy cultures continually challenge their assumptions. That work can seldom be done by one person sitting alone in a room: It requires leaders who listen to others. An oft-told story about Motorola® during its heyday in the 1980s concerns a young middle manager who approached then-CEO Robert Galvin and said, "Bob, I heard that point you made this morning, and I think you're dead wrong. I'm going to prove it: I'm going to shoot you down." When the young man stormed off, Galvin, beaming proudly, turned to a companion and said, "That's how we've overcome Texas Instruments' lead in semiconductors!" During that period, there were no rewards at Motorola for people who supported the status quo; managers got ahead by challenging existing assumptions and by pointing out imperial nakedness. In later decades, the company lost those good habits. Alas, sustaining a culture of openness is even harder than creating one.

Practice having unpleasant conversations: As beneficial as openness may be, great, but unintentional, harm can come from people speaking honestly about difficult subjects. That's why managers find it so hard to give performance appraisals to subordinates whose work is not up to par. And since offering negative feedback upward— to one's boss—is even more difficult, and understandably so, that occurs even more rarely. There is no way to make giving feedback fun for the bearer of a bad assessment or for the recipient.

But Northrop Grumman found a way to teach executives to handle it gracefully. The company's recently retired chief ethics officer, Frank Daly, established a program wherein managers can practice having unpleasant conversations. It helps them learn how to deliver negative messages constructively, without being hurtful. The good news is that such exercises appear to be increasingly common in large corporations.

Diversify your sources of information: Leaders have to work hard to overcome the tendency to lock themselves up, figuratively speaking, in hermetically sealed C-Suites. They should remind themselves of the secret that all well-trained journalists, consultants, and anthropologists learn: When you're setting out to understand a culture, it's best to seek diverse sources of information that demonstrate a variety of biases. This is a simple and obvious point, but rare is the leader who regularly meets with—and listens to— employees, reporters, shareholders, regulators, and even annoying critics.

Admit your mistakes: Wise leaders do this. It once was said about Gandhi, "He makes no compromise to admit having been in the wrong." And President Obama's admission during his third week in office—that he'd "screwed up" by appointing top officials who had played fast and loose with the IRS—sets the contemporary standard for how executives should right their mistakes. Admitting that you've goofed not only disarms your critics but also makes your employees more apt to own up to their own failings.

Build an organizational architecture that supports openness: This task begins with creating norms and structures that sanction truth telling. Such organizational practices as open-door policies, ombudsmen, protection for whistle-blowers, and internal blogs that give voice to those at the bottom of the hierarchy can help. Ethics training can also be useful, although too much of it in corporations is "CYA" (cover your actions) legal compliance.

The executive selection process is potentially the most powerful institutional lever for cultural change, because the tone is set by those at the top. As we have seen, transparent behavior is unnatural among those in positions of power. In fact, executives are seldom chosen for their ability to create a culture of candor. The habit of listening to contrarians is not a trait that most companies or executive recruiters seek in future leaders. Most of the time, they're selected not for their demonstrated teamwork, but for their ability to compete successfully against their colleagues in the executive suite, which only encourages the hoarding of information.

Changing that system is the responsibility of boards of directors. Truly independent boards would go a long way toward providing a needed check on executive ego and a source of objective truth telling. Errant executives will not begin to act virtuously as long as boards continue to reward their misbehavior. Raytheon's® board, for example, recently claimed that promoting ethical behavior was a criterion it used in setting executive bonuses.

Yet shortly after the company's CEO admitted that he had plagiarized large parts of a book he claimed to have written himself, the board voted him a $2.8 million bonus. When pressed, a Raytheon spokesman explained that ethics was just one factor the board had considered. Boards are the last line of defense against ruinous self-deception and the suppression of vital truths. If they're not vigilant in the pursuit of honesty, the organizations they serve are unlikely to have a free internal or external flow of information.

Set information free: Corporate managers tend to keep a great deal of information private that could easily—and usefully—be shared widely. For the past 20 years, every employee at SRC Holdings®, a diversified remanufacturing company, has had access to all financial and managerial information, and each is taught how to interpret and apply it. The net effect, in the words of the company's CFO, "is like having 700 internal auditors out there in every function of the company." The firm has extremely high ethical standards and has been a financial marvel, generating impressive profits, creating jobs, and spinning off new businesses sustainably year after year.

As this example illustrates, extensive sharing of information is critical to both organizational effectiveness and ethics. That's why exemplary leaders encourage, and even reward, openness and dissent. They understand that whatever momentary discomfort they may experience is more than offset by the fact that better information helps them make better decisions. Unfortunately, there is no easy way to institutionalize candor. Honesty at the top is the first step, but true transparency, like a healthy balance sheet, requires ongoing effort, sustained attention, and constant vigilance.

How can we can package that information and enable organizations to drive it and have it readily available for everybody to use? If it's presented in such a way that the employee cannot understand clearly, it is of no use.

Sharing information applies to more than allowing employees to access it. In some instances, it involves providing full access to competing companies. One might wonder why a company would even consider making the results of its research and development available to its competitors. Tesla offers a good example. Tesla started building amazing batteries for cars that drive 240 miles on a charge—the batteries had a great patent, and a positive effect on the environment. But the way Tesla CEO Elon Musk put it is that, if one looks at the penetration of electric cars worldwide, it's apparent that not many people are buying them. There aren't many charging stations in the world to charge electric cars. Holding those patents to their chest didn't enable anybody else to innovate around that process. The issue of increased market share for electric cars wasn't just about the cars themselves, but also about creating the eco-system to support them.

Tesla opened up their patents, and by doing so there are going to be more car companies building electric cars. Concomitant to that is the buildout of the eco-system needed to support electric cars. Think about it, when the gasoline car first came out, there wasn't a gas station on every corner. The whole business of gas stations grew because the number of gasoline-fueled cars on the road increased. By opening up their patent, Tesla is helping the whole electric car movement, as well as the environment and an eco-system is being built around them.

From a legal standpoint, a culture of open information is a different kind of licensing. The licensing that governs Linux right now is a public governance. It basically states that an individual or company is free to use this product under this license however they see fit, but anyone using the product has to share the ways in which they're using Linux with other in the Linux community. We have to get away from the whole process of patents, where somebody holds it for a certain amount of time. For example, look at Keurig®, the coffee maker. It was when their patent expired that the Keurig revolution actually took off, because other companies began making the coffee cups, which helped Keurig sell more coffee machines.

You can be a small player and hold onto your patents, or you can be a big player and let your access to your intellectual property help your invention to grow and innovate in gratifyingly unanticipated ways.

The open-source movement also emerged from this philosophy of users utilizing a product however they see fit. Red Hat® was one of the companies that embraced the open source from Linux, and they became the one of the largest companies in the world of driving.

The Linux kernel was developed by someone. They put the source code out there and said: *You're free to do whatever you want to do with this kernel.* Red Hat picked up that kernel, and started innovating and building structures on top of that original kernel. They created their own version of the Linux Operating System and put it on servers and desktops. Then people started using it and driving it. They are governed by the whole GNU license. So one can always go and look at every single line of code that they have. One can't do that with Microsoft's Window codes because it's all proprietary. Red Hat was able to build a huge company around that whole open source, without having to hide any of the code and the information that they have.

What drives their revenue are the services, which continued to increase as a revenue stream. Linux's source code is open, and if somebody puts in a back door, it's open for the world to see, and they can always start talking about it and take it out. That was the advantage that Linux had over everybody else, because everybody knew there were no back doors— they could see the code and nothing was hidden.

The open-source movement isn't restricted to software. It is applicable to all industries. One is the gene-sequencing process referred to earlier in this book. What other areas can you think of where the open-source Movement could benefit an entire industry?

The old thought process was this that in order to protect something, you had to guard it closely, and not share it. The issue right now is that everything has become so complex that no one organization can keep up with the pace of the innovation. One needs to employ parallel processes in order to maintain a competitive edge. In this way, the open source process helps you become more competitive and you can put the right structure around it.

That's what we call the share or the IP share. It doesn't mean that you're giving it away. It means that you're inviting people to help you build it. The benefits are obvious—naturally, you will be able to tap into a far greater number of creative minds, and in the end, you will also have access to the new and improved product.

In some ways, the software industry is different from older industries. The software world revolves around the sharing of information. However, older industries can adapt some of the practices being utilized in that industry.

Thanks to technology, this will most likely change distribution models. Whereas older industries were aimed toward physical distribution, the emphasis is now on digital distribution. However, if you look at today's 3D printers, that's changing, as well. I suspect we'll evolve to an age where consumers don't really have to go to the store to buy anything—but be able to download and create their purchase. In fact, in some industries, this is already possible.

The collaboration we're seeing between organizations on distribution also enhances competitiveness. Zappos is a perfect example. Their cross-communication on their consumer data really helped their suppliers to understand Zappo's customer trends, and helped meet their customers' marketplace needs. Prior to that, as manufacturers, suppliers didn't interface with end customers and really didn't understand what was going on in the consumer side. They had to rely on Zappos to tell them what they needed.

When Zappos began to share consumer data with them, manufacturers could then increase their pre-planning and have a more predictable process. This enables them to help Zappos stock the products and materials they need more quickly. This supply-chain efficiency also helped Zappos to increase its customer-satisfaction rating. More consumers gravitate to Zappos because they know they always get what they need on the first try, and don't have to wait for it. There is more interactivity across the entire supply-chain process.

Java® is a platform-neutral process. If you have a browser that has Java on it, anybody can create any type of an application within Java, and they don't care if you're using a Firefox®, Internet Explorer®, or Safari browser®. Whichever one you're using, you can always get to the Java data to work.

It wasn't long ago that applications were created for just one thing, such as for Internet Explorer. If someone walked in with an Apple computer or a Linux computer, they couldn't use it, because it was very platform dependent.

In this example, those applications didn't cater to some customers and may have alienated them, because of technology issues. Now that most applications are being Web based, taking away the pieces that would inhibit one's customers from sharing platform information helps, instead of hinders, a company.

The closer we get to the platform-neutrality process, the easier it is. Again, it's all about the content. It's not about how you're getting to that content. That's why smartphones are omnipresent. They enable users get to the content they want on the type of device they have. It doesn't matter if it's an iPhone or an Android. They don't have to rush out and buy a different smartphone in order to access certain information. It's not about the device, it's about having a platform that conveniently offers information in different formats.

The initiative towards open standards for platform-neutral communications is really just a different take on old ways of doing business. In the old days, consumers had the telephone and the fax. It didn't matter what brand the fax machine was, everyone could send and receive faxes. It didn't matter what brand of handset was sitting on your desk, you were always able to get a phone call from someone and answer the phone. It was a platform-neutral process that enabled this.

Now, we're getting to a point where our devices are becoming platform neutral. We have to get to that open structure and open platform so people can innovate on top of those base platforms.

If you look at the other side of it, available carriers include Verizon®, AT&T®, and T-Mobile®. However, you can't buy a Verizon phone and connect it to AT&T. It doesn't work because they use different technologies and different platforms. This forces the consumer to go buy another phone and sit the old phone from the competing carrier on a shelf because they can't do anything with it.

Again, it's not about the devices. We have to get to a point where, with so many open standards in the world, we'll be able to connect anything to anything, which will allow the open process and free flow of information between these devices.

Google and Android have been successful in this new culture of information. It doesn't matter what brand of phone you have, it runs on an Android operating system, and you can download apps and it always works.

On the other hand, there is Apple and the iPhone. If you have an iPhone, you can only go to the Apple store to download apps that are specifically made for iOS. You're basically tied in to an iPhone that you can only buy from one place, which is Apple. Apple has a lot of money, and they're tremendously innovative. However, their innovation isn't anywhere near the innovation we're seeing with the Android. If Apple had more companies sharing information, they would have a lot more firepower than they do by themselves.

The Linux process is really community-centric—geared toward the communities that are built around Linux and people who spend hours and hours of their own time, unpaid, contributing to Linux's code and ~~to~~ making it into a better operating system. This is why Linus is a system that's running 90% of the servers of the world, versus Microsoft, which only Microsoft coders and employees are allowed work on.

Free Open Source Software (FOSS)

Free Open Source Software (FOSS) was a movement that started a number of years ago within the software community and enables them to move the structure into a format where people will be able to use the software, look at the source code, and make additions to develop it.

FOSS for us has been around for quite some time and has been very successful. There have been a number of products that have come out of it. In the cloud environment, one of the biggest uses of FOSS is Docker®, which is basically a virtualized environment of software within a container sitting on a number of servers across the world. Companies like Microsoft and Amazon have started adapting to Docker and becoming more involved in the FOSS program. One of the top Microsoft engineers recently announced that they might open source Windows—a major announcement. Most companies in their industry are looking at going to that platform because no one company can afford not to develop in that open-source format. An open source format results in thousands and thousands of free codes coming from different parts of the world on the Internet, and no one company can compete with that type of coding power.

The biggest piece in monetizing FOSS is in the services around it. The best way to explain this is when you're looking at a taxi service, you're not monetizing on the car, you're monetizing on the service that is being provided with that car. Now, if somebody came out and created an app, that app itself doesn't do anything. Instead, it is based on the services around it. People pay for that service in order for the convenience of using that app. It's the same model for FOSS. Docker software is free, but anybody who provides services within Cloud can charge for using those servers and everything else around it. The code gets better each day, and they monetize based on the services around the software. The old model of looking at software as an asset is going away, and that software is becoming an enabler for services. That's the new business model.

Apple gives out free Mac software. They used to charge for the software, but they no longer do. When you went from Windows 95 to Windows Vista, you had to buy that package. Well, Windows 10 is no longer doing that, and Windows 10 is also going to be free.

Business and the Internet are moving in this direction. It's becoming more of a service-oriented structure. A number of years ago the industry started the service-oriented architecture, and then moved into a cloud environment, and it became more of a service and pay as you go. Today, with Amazon Cloud Drive or any cloud services, you don't pay for the hardware. You're not buying hardware, nor buying software. S, the monetization comes from the services that you're providing, versus selling a product.

FOSS brings that piece together that enables us to not spend a lot of money on the asset itself, and not spend a lot of money on developing software because the software is free. It's open and everybody can use it, and develop a service around it. It's like somebody giving you a free car, and you're driving it around to make money by being a chauffeur or delivery person.

In my opinion, FOSS is going to be dominant in the market. Another good example is Chromebooks®, which are gaining traction against personal computers (PCs). Their success is service driven. Chromebooks are designed as a gateway to the Web. They aren't necessarily a PC that has a big hard drive and a lot memory. Chromebooks are relatively cheap. Then how does Google make money from them? Through all of the services Google provides and the advertising they secure. They don't make money on the Chromebooks themselves.

Chrome OS is actually being developed in a FOSS format. So, there's a chromium process that is in the background. That's an open-source software. You can download the Chrome OS if you want, then install it on your machine for free. That gives you the same environment that you can get on Chrome OS, and it's basically a gateway to Google services.

When you log in to a Chrome OS, you're basically logging into a Google environment. So, if you want to use video chat, you use Hangouts on Google. If you want to use email, you use Google's email service, Gmail. If you want to create documents, you're using Google's online Web doc. So the model differentiates itself from antecedents like Microsoft, which would sell you a PC and the operating system that goes on it. Then, Microsoft would sell you an Office package to put on your computer. By the time you're done with a relatively small PC, you would have spent $1,500 to $2,000 on the computer hardware and the software to use it. With the Google environment you only spend the $200 for Chromebooks, and you get all of the other services needed to operate it from within the Google environment—many are free, and Google directly charges customers for some of them. Google makes money by the number of people who come to their site with advertisements and search engines. It's data mining.

These days, people don't really look at data mining as a big process. However, Google categorizes all of the things that you do with their services, and they create trends and processes and sell that data to consumer-product companies. The consumer wins because it's a gateway. They get services for free. They get a small PC at an inexpensive price and all of the tools they need to operate it. At the same time, Google makes money. For Google and the consumer, it's a win-win.

Information is power. The more people know, the more people understand, and the better their working environment, the better their decision-making process. Bringing that information and environment together to the lowest level enables people to understand what is going on and why they're doing what they're doing. With millennials entering the workforce, that is the new culture they've helped to usher in. The old culture of *I'm going to tell you what to do, and you just do it* doesn't work for the new age of social networking and a generation that has the need to always be in the know.

Search engines have given us the power to look up and search for anything and everything we need in our lives. And Google is one of the biggest information engines in the world. Be it in politics, business, or their everyday lives, when people don't understand something, they go to Google and try to figure it out. Conducting a Google search has become entrenched in everyday culture. Making information transparent to employees who are part of today's knowledge-driven culture allows them to see how their contributions are impacting and transforming their company, and gives them the sense of gratification that comes from being part of something much bigger than themselves.

Now, obviously, if you're doing something wrong, that philosophy doesn't work, but for most US companies that are trying to be more innovative, a more socially responsible company, this process will really help them, because once something comes out against that company, all of the employees in that company are in the know and they can rebut that process.

5

CULTURE OF

SPEED

"The world is changing very fast. Big will not beat small anymore. It will be the fast beating the slow."

Rupert Murdoch

THE NEXT FACTOR IN THE CULTURE OF OPEN IS SPEED. MY definition of speed is understanding how fast one can get something to market. A lot of companies talk about ROI (return on investment), but ROI doesn't mean anything if you don't test the speed behind getting it in the market at the right time and at the right clutch.

Let's use smartphones as an example. There were a number of companies that actually had the smartphone idea and tried to bring it to market, BlackBerry being one. But, they couldn't bring it to market fast enough, and Apple became the de facto, default for that particular product. Now, when you talk about smartphones, the first thing that comes to mind is the iPhone. Speed is the tool to get you to become the market leader before everybody else.

People expect speed. It's not something that is a luxury anymore—it's practically viewed as a right. We live in a high-speed, 24/7 world. If we want to pay our bills at three o'clock in the morning, we get on a computer, pull up our online banking, and do what we need to do. The days of waiting until the bank opens and driving to the branch in the morning are over.

In a corporate culture, speed becomes essential. As a company, making information transparent, and enabling and empowering the employees helps bring your goods and services to market faster. Now everybody understands why they're doing what they're doing. They understand the urgency process and why speed matters. They know why they're asked to work until 10 o'clock at night and why doing so will make a difference.

To facilitate speed, there must be a real understanding of the environment. Along with our demand for speed and immediate information, there is a need for authenticity and transparency. For instance, the Internet opens the door for a business to be open 24/7, 365 days a year. But what if you're a small business and you receive a complaint or inquiry on a major holiday, when you're not officially open for business?

Because speed is vital to the customer's satisfaction, one must account for those occasions, so the customer doesn't feel neglected. Autoresponders are one way to do that, giving the company the ability to reply, stating they will receive a response within 24 to 48 hours.

When there's a vacuum, people begin to view your business and customer service as less efficient—and at times, even inferior—to that of your competitors, and even non-competitors. The bar and expectations for rapid-fire customer care has been raised very high. For that reason, speed must be integrated into your company's corporate culture. It's about being on top of customers and their needs, as well as at the top of your sector in production, distribution, communication, and innovation.

Along with the concept of how quickly one brings a product or service to market, speed has other meanings. Speed isn't just how quickly customer service or electronic communications are executed, it's part of the culture of a company, and requires changes in the way corporate structures are perceived.

For example, how does innovation happen among company employees, then make its way to the C-Suite level, and get implemented? How does that innovation then become a product, and how long does the entire process take? At the same time, that speed process will help keep people informed, through the dissemination of information to the people and making sure they understand the formation. Remember, when people don't hear, they don't know. When they don't know, they adapt a negative perspective on an issue. They never think that the person that hasn't responded might have a satisfactory explanation, and think "Oh, this person is busy—they'll get back to me tomorrow." The first thing they think is, "He doesn't like me. He doesn't want to respond to me." It always seems to move toward the negative, versus the positive.

A company needs to be transparent not only with good information and news, but also with the bad. If a company is having problems, being transparent really helps in the process. Let's look at the example of a supplier to a company that is experiencing supply-chain issues. If you're transparent with your customers and say, "Sorry for the delay. This is the problem. We're going to need to do XXX," the customers are a lot more understanding than if they don't get a full explanation from you on the drivers of the delay, and keep hearing that they're going to get the product tomorrow. Then, tomorrow comes and your company has to admit it has an ongoing problem. This harms your company's credibility and image. Be transparent and ultimately share what the issue is, followed with a projected delivery date—one your company feels confident it can fulfill. Your customers might have resources to contribute to you to help you succeed. People want to see other people succeed. Nobody wants to see a business fail, but, if they don't get the information they need and you're not transparent, they will form a different opinion and their own conclusions.

Obviously, there are limitations if your business consistently has supply-chain and delivery issues. However, no business is perfect, and there are always issues that come up. How you deal with that issue and relay that information is what really changes the mindset of your customers. In regard to speed, the sooner you relay the information, the less damaging it will be.

People demand speed, and the business world has responded by expediting industrial and shipping processes, and using manufacturing equipment that can produce with amazing swiftness. Ordering and billing procedures have been streamlined and contribute to the exponential increase in getting faster to market that we are seeing today. The various types of speed all play a factor in the process of being open and transparent. But the most important factor is the speed of the delivery of information.

As previously mentioned, it's the sharing of information that changes your customers' perspective. If an individual orders something online and thinks it's coming from Kansas and will arrive in two days, but it's actually coming from China and it's going to take ten days to get there on a ship, it changes the perspective of that customer. If they know it's coming from China, they'll already have an expectation that it is going to take longer to arrive. So, they won't pick up the phone and call you on day two, saying, "Where's my product?"

When we talk about speed, we're also talking about product innovation and getting your ideas into the market. Let's use the Apple Watch as an example. Apple announced their information, so the speech segment was pretty fast in getting it into the market. They created a cult around the Apple Watch. However, the actual watch had not yet been rolled out, and no one could actually go to a store and purchase one. In this instance, what matters is the speed of getting the information out into the public sphere and building a culture around it. Then, setting expectations on how soon they will be able to purchase the item. That's the other key term: expectation.

This culture involves the speed of getting information out and then setting the expectation of what people should expect with the whole cultural open process. Consumers expect a good product from Apple because that's Apple's history. There is a whole culture consisting of people who don't mind standing in line for three days to get an iPhone because they already know the level of quality and innovation they will be getting—and the phone's new features. That information was communicated to them already Consumers learned from Steve Jobs' product launch how long it was going to take for them to actually get the latest iPhone in their hand, and that there were countless people regionally and globally who also wanted to be the first to own the phone. Setting firm, clear consumer expectations is what has made iPhone rollouts so successful.

I've always said the first person to market wins. I said it at a conference in San Francisco, and one man refuted, saying, "Well, look at Microsoft Word," in reference to MS Word's surge in popularity that ultimately replaced WordPerfect® as the chosen word processing program. I still feel like Microsoft is a winner, but obviously innovation has sped up since then, and it's not a power player like it was 20 years ago. A company's status may decline over time, but the importance of the first-mover advantage still stands.

Speed is very important, but the information that goes along with speed is as important as the speed itself. Speed only helps you when you can get the right information out, and those who receive it understand it and accept it. The Culture of Open aims to help them understand. Sony and their reader is another example. Sony was the first to come out with the electronic reader for a book. They had a bookstore behind it. They had their contracts in place. But, today nobody has ever heard about Sony readers. Nobody even talks about them. They were way before Kindle®. They had the speed to the market, but what they didn't have is the information that goes along with it. They put their e-readers in a few Sony stores, but that was the only place someone could buy them. They never really advertised it or marketed it to people. Two years later, Amazon came along with the Kindle. What did they do differently? They got the information out and made sure people understood what they were getting. One thing Apple has been really good at is giving people something they didn't know they needed until they got it in their hands, which is what Amazon did with Kindle. People really didn't know they needed an e-reader until Amazon introduced it into the market. Yet, Sony had the same product, but it failed to take off. Informing the consumer was the main difference between the success of one and the failure of the other. Going back to Microsoft, Word has been around for a number of years. It was one of the first word processors. But WordPerfect was being used before Microsoft Word. Nobody hears about WordPerfect anymore. They exist, but nobody talks about them. Microsoft pushed WordPerfect out by dominating the desktop-software market.

Today, Word is a great product. It does a lot of things, but it's data heavy. It requires a pretty good-sized PC or Mac to run it. What consumers are gravitating toward now is next-generation word processing capabilities, like Google Docs. Google has created the environment for Microsoft to put Word online.

You can use a Chromebook to use Word online. This is why Microsoft is really starting to move away from dominating the desktop, because the desktop is not a desktop anymore. It's a gateway. Windows was designed to be a one-person system, which is why it's called the PC, the personal computer. It was never designed to be on a network at work to support collaboration. You can't do that with Microsoft Word on your desktop. Then what happened? Google came across with Google Docs, and now you can collaborate with other people.

It was speed and being the first to create, market and launch the concepts behind these products that brought them to the forefront in the marketplace.

In order to be most effective, speed shouldn't pertain to any one thing—it should be a company's culture. The collaboration process enables people to work faster. It's so much faster and better to be able to get online and collaborate on a document and make changes all at once than it is to email the document back and forth, or to hand someone the original, make copies, and have different copies at different stages floating around.

This expediency enhances communication. The speed becomes both inherent to and a driver of the culture. The more you can develop your employees and the more tools you give them to be more proficient, the greater the cost reduction—based on time reduction.

That changes the whole concept of innovation. It becomes how fast you can be the first to market by enabling people by embedding speed in your company culture. In doing so, you're eliminating frustrations, because in an open-culture company, information is always available and accessible. People are collaborating. Everybody knows what everybody else is doing—if they want to know.

Toyota is a great example. They removed all of the tall cubicle walls that kept people sequestered. They knocked all the walls down so people could see each other, collaborate, and talk. We looked at the new software on the ERP systems. Most of them have a chat function now because that enables speed. Speed enables people to get an idea out, which goes back to our earlier conversation around being the first thing to market and getting information out to market.

For employees, the culture of speed can be either exhilarating or exhausting, depending on the level support. If you try to implement a culture of speed but don't provide support and next-generation tools, you will not yield the desired efficiency. It's kind of like giving someone a three-cylinder automobile and expecting him race against a 700-horsepower race car. It becomes frustrating. Your employees can't keep up. You've have to give them the right tools—and keep updating those tools. You must also help your employees adapt to this new environment.

A lot of people in an older, more established company are not going to adapt easily. And if you don't give them the proper tools, new employees will become exhausted. It's a balancing act between the tools that already exist at your company and the new ones you're replacing them with or integrating.

Speed by itself is not dehumanizing. A production assembly line with people standing like robots doing the same thing over and over becomes dehumanizing. That's why most companies are replacing people on production lines with robots—robots don't get tired. They don't need a break. They can run things much faster, much better, and more efficiently. But enabling speed via a corporate culture that enables employees to bring ideas more quickly to market and improve on the process of how information is shared is not dehumanizing, but a win. Employees get the information they need when they need it, how they need it, and they can interact with each other.

It all comes back to communication. We are social animals. And we live in an age with expanded social options—whether it's on the web using social media or in-person communication. The more social a company makes its corporate culture, the greater speed it will experience. People will know what they're doing and how it fits into their employer's larger vision, and they'll have the tools to get the job done. They'll also have the platforms and options for working more quickly, in pursuit of work-life balance.

Speed is just one element in this process. You can't have speed by itself without all the other elements. They go hand in hand with an open culture and the right tools. It's like having a car, but only focusing on the engine without focusing on the rest of the automobile. The car is going to fall apart, or you're going to get into an accident if it doesn't have brakes. You have to have all of the elements together in order for this process to be successful.

In the matrix, speed is one of elements of the whole structure. There is also the need for information, the open dissemination of the information, the toolset, and how that enables the culture to become more successful. Putting all of those pieces together and pointing it into one spearhead enables innovation and has enablers coming out of it.

How do you incorporate speed into the culture of a company without sacrificing quality or requiring people to work 24/7? How can it be done without placing demands on employees and making them feel like it's a fire drill all of the time? It's really understanding how to build a culture within a company that enables speed. Speed happens as part of the process, and people understand that. Perfection comes with that—you're not sacrificing one for the other.

If we look a company from the 1950s, compared to one today, there has been a huge cultural shift. Even if we look at early 2000 to 2015, in just 15 years there have been many changes. Traditionally, companies have been very slow to adapt these changes and find ways to interact with the environment. As part of the culture of open, it's about understanding what speed is, how you can incorporate that and have a culture that can adapt to the market forces as they happen. The changing forces in the market happen more rapidly than they did years ago. There wasn't much change from the 1920s to the 1950s, but we saw quite a bit of change from the 1950s to the 1970s.

From 2000 and beyond, the speed has picked up because our information gets disseminated faster. Just look at a computer built in 2000 compared to one today. Cell phones are also a great example. Do you remember those big Motorola brick phones that people used to carry? That wasn't that long ago, but today we look at it as ancient. Today, we have people who ask, "How did we ever get anything done without email?" Yet, email is going away, as well, because we're adapting to all of these changes. The ability of corporate culture to adapt to these things at a fast rate speed enables innovation. It enables them to be market leaders and to be able to change with the demand in the market from the consumers who are buying their products.

Speed relates to newness, as well as the standards we have within our cultural norms. For example, a few years ago, there was a big trend around people eating healthy and having access to healthier foods. McDonald's® was among the last establishments that started the process of using grilled chicken in their menu items—they were late to the market in that aspect, and other companies surpassed them. Chipotle® and other companies drove that trend. Not only was McDonald's slow to respond to the health trend, but because of their wide distribution and image, it became very difficult for them to change the public's perception. By invoking a culture of speed, the process would have been faster. The culture of open and the structure we're putting together is how to react to those trends as fast as possible.

Smoking was a big trend in the 50s, 60s, and 70s. RJ Reynolds® was making a lot of money because of that, but they were hurting people as well. Then the cultural anti-smoking trend came in and smoking began to phase out. States started banning smoking in restaurants, bars, and other public places. That trend put a lot of tobacco companies out of business. Now, e-cigarettes are the new trend. The companies that jumped on the trend were able to innovate around it. They found a way to raise money out of the problem, just in a different way. They've created a culture that is be able to innovate around a new trend and respond to the market. Very quickly, e-cigarettes spurred other products, like vapor cigarettes.

The culture of a company doesn't only affect the customers, but it also permeates down to vendors and suppliers. A good example is In-N-Out Burger®, which has one of the highest quality standards in the fast-food industry for their meat. They created a relationship with their suppliers and require certain types of meat in order to meet their criteria. They want that quality, but at the same time they want it fast. Their stores always have a certain amount of supplies on hand, and that supply has to be fresh and have a certain shelf life before it hits their stores. There are only a few suppliers that can meet their demands. If you want to be an In-N-Out burger supplier, your systems have to be fast. In order for companies to compete for that business, they have to adapt the culture of In-N-Out Burger.

Walmart is another example. Walmart is notorious for requiring steep discounts from their vendors. If a company is interested in greatly expanding its distribution, it will more than likely have to deal with Walmart. Vendors don't have a choice but to adapt to Walmart's procurement process. Walmart pushes their vendors every day on pricing, speed, and quality. The slower ones can't keep up, so they fall out of the Walmart vendor pool. That's why when you go to Walmart superstores, you might see a certain type of yogurt for a certain period of time, then all of a sudden, it disappears. It's because they can't keep up with the process that Walmart requires.

Walmart's process is good for the consumers, especially when it comes to their lower prices and expectation of a certain quality. But if you're vendor, it's is very hard to deal with Walmart or even understand how to deal with Walmart. However, if a vendor has openness in their process, Walmart will know exactly what they're going to get, the quality of the product and how it's made, and how fast they are going to get it. The key is to give them that information quickly. Then, even if your product costs more than your next competitor, Walmart may still pick you over the other one.

Walmart understands its market and target audience. A mom-and-pop store, though, cannot play at the same level. They might have aspirations to be on a national level, but have to understand what they're capable of. What is the supply chain or production rate? What are their structures, and how can they take them into the market and build a customer surrounding?

There are some businesses that have been very successful in doing that, Harley-Davidson® being one. While Harley-Davidson is certainly no longer a mom-and-pop brand, their productions have taken off in the last few years, but before that, their motorcycles were very rare and people would be on a waiting list in order to get a Harley. They were willing to do that because it was a Harley, and they knew the quality level they were going to get. Building a culture around your product always helps.

As consumers we have become addicted to speed. Some Android phone users wonder why they don't receive software updates on their phones. That's why Google built the whole Nexus® product line. On the Nexus line, consumers are guaranteed to receive updates as soon as Google releases them. For Samsung and Verizon, it might take eight months to see an update on phones. People don't want to wait. That's one reason why, when Google announced the Nexus 6 at the beginning of 2015, there were backorders for months. Samsung is now catching up on that trend: Consumers don't want to wait for a year to get a software update on their phone because by that time, technology will have evolved and a new phone will come out. In that case, most people would prefer to just buy the new one.

Apple's genius is that it builds a cult around anticipation for their products. If you're successful at building a cult around your product, like Harley Davidson and Apple have done, the level of customer brand loyalty virtually eliminates competition—through fealty alone. People wait for an iPhone because they are Apple fans—and will never buy an Android. It doesn't matter what features or products Samsung offers. Customer commitment is what drives Apple's brand.

One of the advantages Apple has is they are very good at making bad things look good for their people. When they were marketing, they said if you buy an iPhone, you're guaranteed that it won't be obsolete in six months. People saw that as an advantage. But Apple turned that on its head and their marketing department has done a very good job of keeping customers. When the iPhone 5 came out and then six months later, the iPhone 5s, it was seen as a really big mistake because a lot of people were disappointed because they bought an iPhone when a new one was on the market a few months later. Apple still survived, because they have a cult around their product. If you don't have a cult around your product, you cannot afford to make those mistakes because the competitors are going to step on top of you. But if you are dominant in the market and have already established that process, speed comes into play. Speed is what's going to give you that competitive advantage, and Apple is a prime example of using speed to their advantage in the market and as a means to compensate for areas that might have hurt public perception.

A lot of companies focus just on speed without having the other elements behind it. Usually, those are the more traditional companies that are trying to catch up to their competitors, more than trying to actually be in the market and anticipate the market. It's the difference between understanding and trying to predict what the market is going to do, versus being reactive to the market. Samsung is one of the greatest examples of that.

In the beginning, Samsung tried pushing out their phones as fast as possible. They tried to mimic Apple and went into patent infringement until they were able to change and catch up, based on their own internal innovation. It cost them a lot of money and lost customers because their phones weren't good for the generation. Samsung fell asleep behind the wheel, and Apple came in suppressed them pretty fast. Samsung has since learned from that experience, and their products now hold a strong standing among consumers.

BlackBerry is another one that had a dominance in the business market, and they, too, fell asleep behind the wheel. Apple passed them. BlackBerry tried to corner the market with their first touchscreen product. Many felt it was an awful product because they had to rush it into the market in order to compete. This is proof that speed by itself isn't effective—it must have the other elements around it.

As you can see by these examples, the culture of speed by itself without all the other elements actually can be destructive. Having all the elements come together, with speed being part of the process, is what makes it productive.

Speed is not communicated. If we look at a speed by itself, it's not something a company states to its employees, saying we want to be fast. Speed is a natural result of an open culture. It's one of those unspoken things that happens into the culture if you have all the other elements and enablers in place.

Top management has to understand that speed is important, but they can't communicate that. They have to enable people and build a culture around it. It is that culture that will inherently speed up the process. What you can do is to put in a modern application that helps your supply chain. You look at your network optimization process and optimize your supply chain. Speed is the result when you're enabling your people to do things faster.

Speed is the result when they can collaborate. Instead of getting on the phone and talking to each other one at a time, they can go into a chatroom and talk to each other as a group. If the management of a company thinks their company is slow, they have to look for root causes of the slowness because being slow is a symptom of other issues. They have to identify the causes and find ways to improve.

If you have a slow production line, you can't just tell people to work faster. You have to change that production line and minimize some of the wasteful efforts that are going into that product. Then, the production line becomes more efficient.

6

CULTURE OF
LEADERSHIP

*"The leader sees things through the eyes of his
followers ... The leader does not say, 'Get going!'
Instead he says, 'Let's go!' and leads the way.
He does not walk behind with a whip;
he is out in front with a banner."*

Wilfred Peterson, *The Art of Living*

PEOPLE ARE PASSIONATE ABOUT ACTIVISM. THERE ARE TWO types of people that go to work every morning. One gets up in the morning and then moans on Monday morning about going to work and spending eight hours in the office, and waits for five o'clock. The other person looks at Monday as a gift—an adventure—and they're excited about it. The first type of person has no passion, and doesn't understand—or feel—that they're part of a bigger picture. Instead, they're going to work to collect a paycheck. The difference between them and the micro-entrepreneur, a person who owns a home business, is that entrepreneurs work from dusk to dawn. They work until the wee hours of the night because they understand and feel that it's their own business and they ultimately benefit. Most important, they are following their passion. This is their dream, and they become an asset for their product—and an advocate. They advertise it and tell everybody what they do, how they do it, and how they are different than their competitors.

It is the leadership that creates a culture of passion within the company, where every single employee becomes an intrapreneur for the company and is driven by the passion that they can't wait to get up Monday morning just to go to work. That shift in mindset creates a big difference in corporate culture, and also brings innovation and speed. That brings the best out of employees because people are going to give everything they have to that company.

Amazon is a very good example. Amazon started way back in the dot-com era as an online bookstore. Today, you can find everything you can think of at Amazon.com. When Jeff Bezos started Amazon, he chose the name because Amazon is one of the longest rivers in South America, and it encompasses everything from one end to the other. His idea and mind frame were around encompassing *everything*. Amazon is a very different company today than it was when it started. That spirit of entrepreneurship has never left the company. Today, they sell music and online movies. You can buy whatever you want on Amazon. They're even selling services around cloud merchants. They can do that because they keep reinventing themselves, and their employees have the mindset that Amazon can be the world. Their passion for their company is also felt and displayed by their employees.

Look no further than the Kindle Fire, which is the world's most popular e-reader. You can now watch movies on a

Kindle Fire. Amazon has even become an Apple and Google competitor. They keep coming up with new things, and the leadership has created a culture where the employees feel passionate about the company. It is a culture that has permeated from the top down. This spirit of entrepreneurship is encouraged throughout the company.

Google started as a search engine, but now they're selling phones and running wires in a number of studies for Google Fiber. They're making a driverless car. These are the things that makes people believe that they won't be boxed into doing one thing all of the time, which makes them excited about what they might do next. It creates an exciting atmosphere and work environment, where employees don't feel bored and look forward to going to work.

More traditional consumer product companies can do the exact same things that Amazon and Google are doing. However, their machine and culture are not accepting that process. They feel that their company is defined by one product or service and don't want to sway from or expand beyond it. They may keep on providing only that one service or product, and they may make a very good profit from it and be successful. But they create a different culture than employees experience at Google, Apple, or Amazon. It's the culture that makes people excited to go to work for those places. That culture starts with the leadership.

The companies that have been able to build that activism within their companies share information. Their people understand what they're doing and how their role impacts their products and the company as a whole. Information comes freely. Their success is centered around open communication and open information. Employees feel valued and worthwhile.

Let's compare Google with Microsoft. I can imagine that people who work for Microsoft are rarely excited about the type of product they make. They're a software company. There is nothing for them to get excited about.

However, look at the employee who works for Google. He's excited, and everybody is interested in hearing about it and learning what the next big thing in the market is going to be. These companies change your perspective. The openness that is practiced in these companies is what creates that culture. It injects that entrepreneurial spirit into the company. It is the leadership who pushes and reinforces that excitement.

Like it or not, Microsoft's culture came from Steve Ballmer more than anybody else, even Bill Gates. Steve Ballmer was one of those hardcore managers who had a hammer in his hand, and if anybody fell out of line, he slapped them in the head with a hammer. Okay, so he didn't really, but he ruled in an inflexible manner. It took away the spirit and excitement of the company. Microsoft now has a new CEO who is trying to change that culture. He has an uphill battle because that's a big organization, and it's like moving the Titanic. It's not going to be an easy task because they lack openness. Their culture and process are still structured and has permeated the culture of the company. That culture goes to the outside—to the customers and the people they're trying to attract to work for their company. With the right culture, you can attract a high talent of people who can come in and really contribute in a big way to your company.

Netflix is a very good example of that type of a company. When people start working for Netflix, they get an offer letter that tells them they have a role and a place in the company. However, once their usefulness is gone, there is a possibility that the will no longer be needed. People love working for Netflix, and they love being there. They never have to guess when they're going to be laid off. They never have to guess what's going to happen next or if they have job security, because the information is accessible to them and they understand it. If the company opts to stop sending DVDs in the mail, an employee in that division knows there will be a need to reinvent themselves because their division and role will no longer be necessary.

It all starts with passion. It's around commitment from the employees and employees understanding that the company is as committed to them as they are to the company, and that they can be advocates and ambassadors for the company. It doesn't matter how much you invest in marketing plans or TV and newspaper advertisements, nothing can beat the word of mouth. You can see ten different advertisements on TV for a particular product, but if your neighbor tells you that it's not a good product, you're not going to buy it. It doesn't matter how many advertising dollars have been put into marketing it.

If a company has 10,000 employees, that's 10,000 ambassadors for their product. These people have families and friends. Multiples of ten for each one of those employees can be advocates for your product all the way across.

When you're have an open, transparent organization, people can understand the information. When there are problems, people will try to find a way to solve it, versus when people don't know the information and must rely on a few people at the top to make all of the decisions and push it down to the people. In that case, they're not using the talent of the people who are working for them. There is a big difference between an open culture and a closed culture because when people don't know something, they cannot react to it. But, when they are informed in a culture where people are committed to the company, people will stand up and come out of woodwork to help solve a problem.

That's how you identify leaders in the process. They are the people who are willing to step up and really change and help you through the process. These people take ownership of the products they create, as well as the results. Those people are the ones who should get promoted and be valued in the company.

Google is a good example of how an open company builds leadership. Marissa Mayer was one of the top executives at Google before she became CEO of Yahoo. She didn't start as a CEO—she worked her way up. The Google culture enabled her to shine and grow into the process to become a very effective leader.

Activist leaders in an open culture know that they have to understand people and the environment they are operating in. They need to be proactive into the process and understand where their employees' roots are and what their cultural roots are. Dissemination of the information down through the levels is important to make sure they understand what the company's goals are.

IBM started as a US-based company, but now operates around the world. They need to understand the goals of the company as a whole and the values not only in the United States, but in other countries, as well. Knowing the different geographies and how they value those cultures and contributing to the communities of those different countries becomes an important factor of motivation in that process.

This takes deliberate thought, careful communication, deep knowledge, and even personal charisma by a leader with an activist mindset. Take Steve Jobs or Larry Page, for example, who used their leadership styles and structures to create open, innovative companies that had the full support of all. One of the greatest tasks a leader has is to sell the dream of their company—to employees, customers, and stakeholders. Those two did that very well.

A leader has to have a vision of what they're going to be and how they're going to change. What will the company's big picture look like? Jeff Bezos did a very good job of that at the beginning of the company that was selling the Amazon dream. He knew precisely what his company was going to offer in the beginning, but he also knew where he wanted it to go. It's no stretch to say that Amazon has expanded immensely and Bezos' vision has come to fruition.

People want a leader who is confident. People want a leader they will follow, as long as they know that you know where you're going, that you have a strut and a dream. That leader might not even have all of the details, but they do have a goal, and that goal drives the company. Whatever that goal is for that company, the company leader has to have that vision and be able to communicate it down to the lowest levels. Not only do they have to have that vision, but they have to have the excitement and passion for it to spur the same excitement in their employees.

People are always wondering, *What's in it for me?* Leaders have to be able to communicate that message, as well. "If we get here, this is what you're going to get. This is how you're going to enhance yourself. This is how you're going to enhance your resume. This is a bonus or a stock option." They have to understand that they play a part in the process and will be rewarded for it. It's not just about earning a paycheck.

The biggest thing in terms of leadership and how to invite employees to excel is vision. Of course, some people are inspired by money, but most people are very inspired by vision. Then, they don't feel like they're exchanging time for money.

Marissa Mayer is very influential. She understands the whole structure of how people think and what makes people tick. When she first came to Yahoo, she stopped people from working from home, which caused a lot of issues. But at the same time, she was able to manage through that and bring people together and explain to them why the ability to work from home wasn't a good idea. She helped them understand that it wasn't just a mandate coming out of the Ivory Tower. She was very open about why she was making that decision and how she came to it. That openness and culture really helped retain the employees that she wanted to retain. I really commend her for the leadership that she brought in to do that, because it was not an easy thing to do. It was very controversial when it started.

Whether you like him or not, President Obama really has vision and an outlook of where he was going to go and how he was going to get there. This was very important to the structure of his administration and campaign during the two elections. He had a conviction, and he delivered on every promise in phases, even with the opposition he had in the process. It was his vision that won over the voters and gained support in carrying it out.

If there is one thing that makes a leader exceptional, it is humility. They are not ivory tower people. Sergey Brin at Google is an example. We've seen a number of pictures of him on the New York City subways. Then there's the CEO of a company who is worth millions, but drives a 15-year-old Audi to work every day. He didn't change and become somebody he is not. People look at humble leaders as genuine, authentic people. They are who they are, and the position, money, and power don't change that. Because they're humble, they can put their vision in place without people feeling threatened that they are being pushed down from the ivory tower. It's all because they connect with people and care about their people.

Employees of those leaders are going to become activists for the company. They're never going to go somewhere else. They're going to be loyal and provide their support without fail. People don't look at it from a dollars and cents perspective. When you give, you're going to get back more.

It takes confidence to make decisions that involve change, but confidence is not something that you communicate. It is part of a person's overall packaging. It's having a vision you believe in and are passionate about and understanding where you're going and how you're driving a company. It's not shooting from the hip, claiming that what you learned in college is how it's going to be done. While business principles are important, they aren't the defining principles that make a company or its employees stand out. Steve Jobs didn't care what college his employees and leaders went to. Instead, he focused more on people and how they interact. What can they contribute to an organization? That culture started from the top. As a leader, Steve Jobs didn't go to an Ivy League school. However, he was an entrepreneur. He really understood the people connection, partly because

Jobs knew how to inspire and motivate others. He really understood what made people tick, how to surround himself with the right people, and how to make a company successful.

Great people are not only aiming to succeed, but they are also willing to fail. This is nothing new; in fact, pushing past failure has been important to progress since the lightbulb was invents. Thomas Edison was asked how he created the lightbulb. He responded, "By figuring out 999 thousand ways how not to make one." Failure is part of the process. If you're not willing to fail, you're not running the car. If you're not willing to fail, you're probably playing it too safe and may find your competition outpacing your company with new innovations and ideas. Failures are part of the process. Once you fail, though, you can't just stay down. You have to get up, dust yourself off, figure out your next step and move on. It's not about understanding and learning from the past, though you do have to use failure as a learning process in order to weed out what does work and keep what doesn't. But you don't have to dwell on it when you fail. It's understanding what's forward and not losing your vision and your dream.

Having a bigger vision and longevity is what creates profits for shareholders. If you want a longer-term company that's going to succeed and become the next Amazon or Google, you have to think beyond the present and have a vision for the future. Where do you see your company in five or ten years? What products or services will you offer? Will you expand into different products, or even different industries? And how can you make that happen with the support of your employees, customers, are shareholders?

These types of leaders aren't born with this mindset. Any reasonable person who is willing to put the effort into it and accept that failure is part of the process can become a great leader when they understand people and the market. It's all about understanding the environment, and not just relying on spreadsheets and numbers. Spreadsheets and numbers are tricky—they can give a wrong impression. GM is a good example. Prior to their bankruptcy, they were putting out cars and making money for their shareholders. It looked good on paper. But, it didn't stop the company from going bankrupt. Why? A bunch of people with MBAs sat down and just pored over their spreadsheets and looked at their numbers. Those numbers looked good, but the reason was because they were cutting costs in critical areas. Then, there's the fact that nobody was buying GM Cars. At the same time, the German and Japanese were making much better quality cars. The price for that one GM car was higher than the Japanese car, but if nobody buys it, it doesn't do anybody any good. As you can see, spreadsheets and numbers can be deceiving, and they certainly don't reflect the whole, greater picture. A passionate leader understands numbers, but also understands the environment.

The qualities of a leader are trainable and can be emulated. To do so, one must increase one's understanding and be willing to take risks. And they have to be willing to put themselves out there and be vulnerable.

The biggest piece we can learn from Steve Jobs is his uncompromising passion for perfection. Again, we see that passion, and the amount of it, expresses itself in the success of a company and the role of its employees.

Entrepreneurial Cultures

Despite the outside attention they often garner, true entrepreneurial—or one could say intrapeneurial—cultures are rare in large companies. One of their hallmarks, at least in their early days, is that they often feature a single, rogue innovator, a leader who by timing or luck finds him or herself orchestrating a maelstrom of disruption. Think Steve Jobs, Mark Zuckerberg, Carroll Shelby, Stephen Elop, Sergey Brin, or, long ago, Edwin Land at Polaroid. In keeping with the bold personalities that run them, the companies are usually willing to take risks that normal companies would consider off the charts.

Cultures that form in response to these leaders are almost never satisfied with incremental growth, but strive for disruption. They target and attack mature companies like sharks where they are weakest—in their business models. They prey on lethargic industries with outdated practices that can be completely disintermediated. They use the power of emerging and disruptive technologies to reinvent the way products and services are used.

Such companies and their cultures can accomplish historic things. They are the very embodiment of the go-big-or-go-home mentality.

The challenge with entrepreneurial cultures is that they can rely too heavily on the genius of the charismatic leader. His or her singular vision can overshadow everything, often devaluing the ideas of others and fostering an atmosphere of suppression and fear. In fact, the leader can be so difficult to handle that the company grows weary of the struggle and forces him out. One of the more stunning images in Silicon Valley history is that of ousted disk-drive legend Al Shugart driving each morning past the company bearing his name.

And of course, Steve Jobs became the poster child for fired icons after being booted from the first iteration of Apple under John Sculley.

The antidote for this kind of lopsided culture is to empower others. Designate intrapreneurs. Create models and practices that don't just encourage novel thinking but also offer channels and forums to openly challenge leadership. Steve Jobs did this brilliantly in his second term at Apple.

Sergey Brin, the co-founder of Google, may have started as a maverick, but he has settled into being the kind of visionary leader it takes to create and nurture a culture friendly to other entrepreneurs. Like BMW, Brin and his team deliberately established processes to provide the necessary protection for risk takers.

The lesson is that a faltering culture is not a failed culture. Even the biggest and best companies derail occasionally. Like the process of innovation itself, cultures require constant adjustment. Make your culture responsible and responsive to its own actions. Stay conscious. Stay deliberate. Keep iterating, not just on product, but on culture.

CONCLUSION

"One changes always leaves the door open for the establishment of others."

Niccol Machiavelli

IN THIS BOOK, I'VE SHARED MANY EXAMPLES OF CLOSED AND open cultures. The information I've learned throughout the years will help you gain an understanding of what an open culture is and the varying degrees of being open. In addition, you'll be able to identify the benefits of moving in that direction and the process of transforming from a closed to an open culture.

This is the natural evolution of business in today's world. Technology has been the driving force behind transparency. We see it in business, and it particularly plays a major role in the lives of millennials, who utilize technology to share all aspects of their lives. As millennials continue to enter the workforce, their reliance on this transparency and technology will have a huge impact on business processes, as well. As a result, the corporate culture will eventually catch up to the more open life that millennials are living today.

If corporations are going to thrive, even survive, in this environment, they will have to adapt to the Culture of Open. It doesn't have to be a major overnight transformation. There are ways to manage information and draw back the curtains on their culture inch by inch to move in that direction. Tomorrow, and in the future, there will be more transparency and regulatory disclosures, which all require openness. This book will help you to prepare for that, manage it, and use it in a profitable manner.

Being open does not mean you have to expose everything. It does mean you want people to understand your business practices and how you do business. This invites you to improve and operate in a way that stands up to scrutiny and earn the trust and respect of your employees, vendors, customers, suppliers, and your industry. Being open is about being a contributor—contributing to innovation and giving people the information they need to be better.

I will venture to say that the openness and sharing of information is good for everyone. In my experience, an open culture has the opportunity to produce success in nearly every company.

After reading this book, I hope you walk away with a better understanding of what open means today and what the future of open entails. With this information, I hope you've learned how to prepare and how to best move forward to open your culture, step by step. By taking those steps and going into the process of why you should open up your organization's culture, you'll discover the benefits doing so brings, and what it means to be responsible for your actions. This process may feel naked—naked is not necessarily bad in this process; it will help you advance and help others trust you.

When you get started down the open-culture path, you may be tempted to give up. In fact, this will happen over and over along the way. Open cultures are often hard. They're not immediately intuitive, and they're likely not comparable to any of the companies you've worked in before. Not only that, open cultures raise endless problems—issues that would normally remain hidden under the surface for months (eventually resulting in people quitting) tend to rapidly bubble to the surface in a transparent culture. This is good, because then you can solve them, but it's also bad, because you feel like there are constantly new problems arising.

Knowing that there are other companies doing this, and being able to adapt ideas from them, is invaluable in this journey.

Yes, there will be growing pains, but there will also be immeasurable rewards. Information technology is changing all aspects of our lives, and the old ideas of privacy and personal versus corporate space are becoming outdated. One step at a time, you can knock down the barriers of brick walls and replace them with glass walls of transparency. The process is an evolution, and I hope you, too, find the journey to be enlightening.

ABOUT NICK BERG

An executive-level strategist with over 20 years of innovation and global business experience, Nick Berg advises C-level peers on the impact of particular people, processes, and technology solutions for the corporation as a whole. He believes true value is the fluency in both business and technology. As a business process improvement consultant, Berg advises Fortune 500 companies on cultural and business transformation.

www.cultureofopen.com

Made in the USA
Lexington, KY
05 April 2016